MW00826903

THE
GANSEY KNITTING
SOURCEBOOK

THE GANSEY KNITTING
SOURCEBOOK

150 STITCH PATTERNS AND
10 PROJECTS FOR GANSEY KNITS

Di Gilpin & Sheila Greenwell

DAVID & CHARLES

www.davidandcharles.com

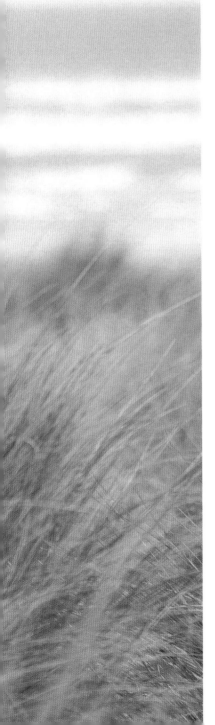

CONTENTS

INTRODUCTION

The Gansey Knitting Sourcebook has been a long time in the making. I first realised how incredible these garments were as a young child on a visit to Whitby in Yorkshire with my dear Aunt Doris, who introduced me to knitting and took me to the Shepherd's Purse yarn store aged 12 to choose some wool and to buy a knitting book. I came away clutching Gladys Thompson's *Patterns for Guernseys, Jerseys & Arans: Fishermen's Sweaters from the British Isles*!

I grew up in East Yorkshire and at one time lived in a house beside the harbour in Bridlington. In a flat in the basement was a retired sea captain, his wife, a parrot and their beautiful Bernese mountain dog. I was six at the time and fascinated to listen over a pot of tea to tales from a life lived to the full on the ocean. I would spend hours fishing for crab off the harbour walls, swimming in the oh-so-cold North Sea and practising my knitting. One of the first projects at school was a pair of gloves on double-pointed needles. When I met Sheila, who is the co-author of this book, our love of knitting on a 'set of 5' double-pointed needles or on long straight needles, with one tucked under the arm, in the Scottish or Northern English way, was a major binding force. Knitting in the round on long double-pointed needles is one of the defining elements in good Gansey knitting!

As lifelong knitters with a special interest in Gansey knitting, we will be taking a journey through the history and special knitting details of these fascinating garments; tension (gauge), stitch counts, patterns, construction details, yarns, colours and motifs. There is a huge story to tell and a lot of history to discover. I worked for many years on the Moray Firth Partnership Gansey Project and this special collection is now at the Scottish Fisheries Museum, where we are currently working on the museum's 'Knitting the Herring' project, leading towards establishing a National Gansey Collection for Scotland that will link with collections from England and Cornwall. We have also included the special Eriskay Ganseys from the Western Isles within the collection.

Bringing together and creating a national collection will enable us to have greater understanding about the origin of the craft and about the makers, many of them women, in the fishing villages around our coastline. It will show us variations between communities and families, whilst illuminating the life of the 'herring girls', proficient Gansey knitters who travelled around the coast, following the shoals of herring, gutting and salting at each harbour as the catch was brought in.

Ganseys are incredibly special. They are knitted seamlessly, traditionally on five long, steel double-pointed needles, in the round using a 5ply worsted-spun Gansey wool, often with false side seams. Knitters created their own patterns, often adding signature stitches that helped define their family or even the village where they originated along the coast of Scotland, England, the Netherlands and

more. These special Gansey stitches are all made from the simple knit and purl stitches, or in the dialect of the Dales in Yorkshire "hit and missitt" (as explained by Mrs Crabtree of Dent in *The Old Hand-Knitters of the Dales* by Marie Hartley and Joan Ingilby). Traditionally Ganseys are constructed in such as way as to allow fishermen unrestricted movement in their work, while also remaining tight fitting with shorter length sleeves to avoid anything getting caught in the nets, hooks and rigging. To facilitate this fit on such hardwearing garments, Ganseys are worked in a very tight gauge with specific features to enhance movement and allow for future repair. These include underarm gussets, a false side seam, shoulders joined - sometimes with a strap or saddle, neck bands often including a neck gusset, and sleeves that are picked up and worked from the shoulder down to the cuff.

In this book Sheila and I hope to explore some of the latest findings in our search for the source of the Gansey, including a study of one family's collection from the north east of Scotland with previously unpublished notes from the knitters going back through the generations. We have also created an incredible archive of the motifs, seeding patterns and fabric designs as a source for knitters to develop their own patterns and to understand the complexity and beauty of these incredible garments, which represent the harmony between the utilitarian and art.

A SHORT HISTORY OF GANSEYS

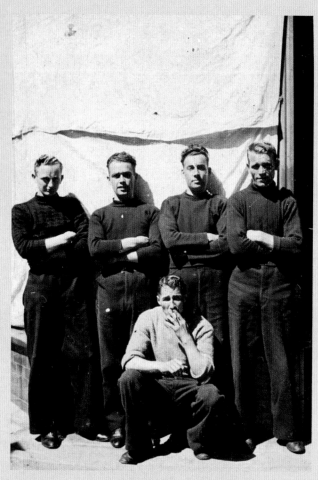

Group portrait of five Pittenweem fishermen.
Image courtesy of the Scottish Fisheries Museum, SFM_4567

WHY GANSEY?

A Gansey is a fisherman's sweater. The name is often linked to Guernsey or Jersey, where there is a history of simple knitted frocks dating back to the fifteenth century. In Gaelic it is known as 'Geansaidh' and in Norwegian 'Genser', another derivation of the generic Guernsey.

The Gansey is knitted seamlessly by hand with gussets and other features, not made by a machine or sewn together in parts. The Gansey is also patterned, rather than stitched in stocking (stockinette) stitch and has a unique tension (gauge) which makes for a dense and wearable garment.

Like many forms of work clothing, the Gansey is perfectly attuned to its job. Many fishing communities lived in remote areas often aligned with sheep and wool. Wool is the perfect material for use in a cold, wet environment as it keeps the body at a regular temperature and, with the dense nature of the Gansey knitted fabric, it repels water whilst keeping the wearer warm.

The complex patterning and particular tension (gauge) of the Gansey suggests it has a long textile history that has developed over many hundreds of years. It has certain similarities to the damask silk knitting documented by Richard Rutt in his book *A History of Handknitting*. Thanks to so-called herring 'quines' (girls and women who helped with the herring catch) such as Mrs Isabella Stewart (see *Undiscovered gems*), we now know families wrote notes to describe and record stitches and patterns, well before any publications of Gansey patterns, although, undoubtedly, hand knitters are curious and would have happily added to their repertoire if they saw something new and interesting. By handling and evaluating the wonderful garments in the collections at the Scottish Fisheries Museum we have been able to further record the complexity of design and construction, which reflects an extremely old knowledge, often overlooked by textile historians. The Gansey is a living document of codes and stitches to be read, and secrets to be unlocked.

Crew of drifter, 'Just Reward', KY239.
Image courtesy of the Scottish Fisheries Museum, SFM_2280

Herring gutters and curers, Anstruther, 1909.
Image courtesy of the Scottish Fisheries Museum, SFM_1879

'Herring quines': the herring trade and 'fisher lassies'

From the 17th century the fishing around the coast of Britain was led by the herring, or 'silver darling' as the wee fish became affectionately known. The shoals of herring collected at the far north of Scotland every year and travelled south through the North Sea. The Scottish Herring Fleet gathered in the Shetland Isles and followed the shoals, catching and then landing the catch as they moved south.

The fishing boats came from all over, including the Netherlands and even further afield. The Museum on Shetland has a fine collection of photographs of skippers, crews and boats taken by the local photographic studio, which capture the men in their fine Ganseys. In the Moray Firth collection we found not just Ganseys, but hand knitted all-in-one long johns (long underwear), worn beneath the oiled trousers, sometimes in a softer pink 5ply wool, but also additional sweaters in a chunkier wool worn as an extra outer layer. It is not easy, however, to decipher the patterns knitted in the regular dark indigo blue in a photograph!

For the fishermen, the only way they had to preserve the herring, a very soft flesh fish that deteriorates quickly once caught, was in vast salt barrels. The fish needed to be gutted, descaled and put into the barrels as quickly as possible. The women who did this came from many different areas of Scotland, including the poorer Western Isles and the north of Scotland, as Isabella Stewart did, and were known as 'herring quines' or 'herring girls'. They travelled with the fleet as they moved south. On some boats the fishermen's wives would do the salting, while other boats hired girls at different ports. Many of the women travelled together and some ended up staying when

Herring gutters at work in Craig's yard, Dunbar, 1930s.
Image courtesy of the Scottish Fisheries Museum, SFM_4075

they reached the end of the journey, some in Edinburgh, others much further south. It was hard, cold and tough work. They wrapped their fingers in cloths to help protect them from the salt and fish scales. Many women knitted on the journey and, I am sure, shared patterns as they went. In many ways this explains how patterns spread from region to region even before the publication of Gladys Thompson's book *Patterns for Guernseys, Jerseys & Arans* in 1971 from material collected during the 1950s.

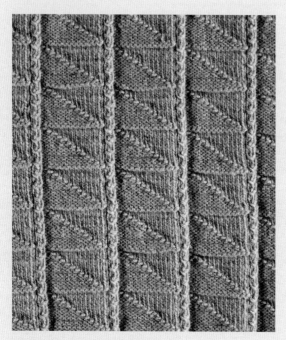

Flags and mock cables, Fraserburgh.
Scottish Fisheries Museum Collection, ANSFM:2019.374

Open diamonds with double 2-stitch mock cables, Fraserburgh.
Scottish Fisheries Museum Collection, ANSFM:2019.377

There are some great books written about Ganseys and we didn't really want to go through the areas of history already recorded, but instead chose to look at some case studies to illustrate the nature of the Gansey and how it sits with the social history of the knitters who made them.

In understanding the Gansey the first and most important aspect is to clarify who the knitter was. During our research with both the Moray Firth and Scottish Fisheries Museum collections, we were able to clearly see the hands of the different makers, their character and resourcefulness. Most of the Ganseys we have looked at were knitted by mothers, wives or daughters for fisherfolk of the family as a protective, important workwear layer worn in one of the most dangerous jobs in Britain. The tension (gauge) for some of the garments was as dense as sixty stitches to 10cm/4in, with complex patterning and construction to make it fit tightly to the body for safety.

The beauty of these garments and the hours taken to make, repair and alter them reflects a love and bond between these families from small villages dotted around the coast. One of our favourite knitting superstars has to be Mrs Elsie Buchan, whose work we have handled in the museum and recorded. Elsie was a tremendous knitter, from Peterhead, in the far north east of Scotland, with fabulous clear stitchwork and a wonderfully inventive mind. Her use of her own two-stitch mock cable as a seeding device (to divide the main designs but also to add or reduce width for a better fit) is beautifully done.

In some instances she has two cables side by side with a two-row twist, in others she inserts a purl stitch between cables and increases the twist to four rows. Each garment is a little different but with her own mark stamped onto it.

The fineness of her work can be seen in two particular Ganseys. The first a Scottish Flag design with a single two-stitch cable twist between. The second, an open diamond with a double 2-stitch cable twist between, which creates a fabulous all-over fabric pattern.

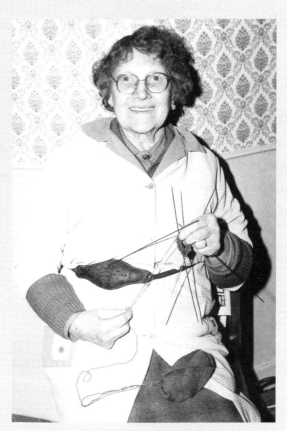

One of Bella's notes for 'The Wave' found in the hand-written files. When knitted up by Sheila, the instructions produced a beautiful pattern

Bella with her 'whisker and wires' (knitting sheath/belt and needles)

Undiscovered gems

Some years ago while working at the Loch Ness Knitting Festival in Inverness, Stephanie Hoyle, who worked for years on the Moray Firth Gansey Project, rushed over with a huge grin on her face. Someone had just presented her with a box of Ganseys we had not seen before... We opened the box and found, not only a number of beautiful garments but a file of hand-written notes!

This felt like an enormous find of real importance: original primary source material to show how patterns were written on scraps of paper and kept, sometimes in favourite books, to be passed down through the family. I managed to trace the person who had brought us the box of Ganseys and notes, Anji, and she sent me lots of information about her grandmother, Bella Stewart, a little of which I have reproduced here.

Isabella Stewart - Gansey knitter and herring quine

Mrs Isabella (Bella) Stewart was born into a fisher family in Seatown, Lossiemouth, in 1902.

As was usual for women of fisher families, she learned to knit. Her mother taught her the skills to knit Ganseys, socks and long underwear, which were all essential garments for the fishermen in the family.

Before marrying James Stewart in 1927, she worked as a herring quine during the herring season. This took her to Great Yarmouth, Barra and Shetland. Her husband, two sons and son-in-law were fishermen, so knitting was part of her everyday life. She was well-known in the community for her Gansey knitting and would often be asked to knit a Gansey for someone else.

Bella continued to knit until she died, at the age of 90, in 1993.

"My Granny - A Gansey Knitter"
by Anji Hancock

"As the daughter of a fisherman in the 1960s I grew up seeing the menfolk in my family wearing Ganseys and knitted woollen socks. The provider of these garments was my paternal grandmother, Isabella (Bella) Stewart. When I think of my granny it's very difficult not to think of her knitting, or 'wyvin' as she would call it. There was always something on her 'wires' (needles) and she took her knitting with her wherever she went.

She always came to visit us on a Friday evening and as a child I was fascinated and a little scared of those long, silver, metal, sharp-pointed instruments that she manipulated skilfully in the process of knitting her latest Gansey. At the end of the row the freed needle would be thrust into her abdomen in what appeared to be a very dangerous manoeuvre. Of course, no physical harm was done – she was wearing her 'whisker' (knitting sheath/belt)! She always said she couldn't knit without it and, as far as I remember, she always used one. Thinking back, I can only remember her knitting Ganseys and socks. Possibly, she did knit other garments, but Ganseys were definitely her 'thing'. Knitting a Gansey looked so easy to her and I was never aware of her using a pattern. Imagine my surprise when, after she died, I opened a battered old tin, that had come from her house, to find some very well-used pieces of paper with knitting instructions for various motifs, such as hearts, diamonds and cones. Some of these were in other handwriting, and one had the message 'hope you can read my writing' so I can only surmise that she had asked a fellow Gansey knitter for instructions to knit a motif she saw them knitting. I certainly got the impression that she was always looking for little ways to make each Gansey different. I distinctly remember her saying 'I think, for a change, I'll give this one cables on the cuffs', and one of my Dad's Ganseys does have cables on the cuffs!

My grandmother was a Gansey knitter and a herring quine – I have the skills to be neither! I definitely regret never asking her to teach me how to knit a Gansey, but the herring gutting – I am very glad that's not even a possibility these days, however much my granny seemed to remember them as 'happy times'!"

Herring quines travelled quite far during the fishing seasons. Bella worked in Barra, left, and also in Lowestoft, below

Bella's written notes for her original tree motif

The tree sample knitted up by Sheila from Bella's instructions

From Anji's notes we noticed several different pattern writing styles from different periods and Sheila set about knitting up some of these patterns, particularly the older ones. It is extremely rare to find notes like this but it does suggest that families did keep their own favourite patterns safe, even though Anji agrees her grandmother was a great knitter and also picked up ideas from newspapers and magazine patterns too. One motif that Sheila knitted from the notes was a really beautiful tree pattern, an older pattern that stands out as an old and original motif and that is also seen in one of Bella's knitted Ganseys.

Two of Bella's Ganseys had already been donated to the Moray Firth collection, but the remaining twelve had not, so the next stage was to record them for the Museum!

The Gansey knit by Bella featuring her tree motif and an excellent example of a shoulder strap

Pattern origins

Post 1950, one of the Gansey patterns began to be named in various books as 'heapies'. These were the triangular designs we have seen in Scottish Ganseys in the collections we have looked at but also in other areas too. I was interested to discover where the word originated. So many patterns are quite descriptive and representational like trees, diamonds and nets, so where did the 'heapie' fit in?

I set out on a quest to find out. My search took me to an article by Alexander Fenton in a particular dialect from the far north of Scotland known as Buchan. It is a delightful research paper describing rural life and exploring the wealth of words from Buchan:

"As the peats at Auchenderran were cut, they were lifted off the blade and set up in little heapies of three, for drying. Some were barrowed home, but the main lot was taken home with her grannie's horse and cart." I immediately connected this with my time living on the Isle of Skye where I was taught to cut the peat to burn in the fire. Catriona, my neighbour, showed me how to stack the fresh cut peat into triangular stacks to keep the weather off them and to allow them to dry before bringing home for our winter fires and the old stove. The shape of the stack is a 'heapie'. The word describes perfectly these great designs, which emanate from this north eastern shore with peat cutting and a rural life rich in Buchan, Doric or Scots language.

In our research at the Scottish Fisheries Museum, Sheila and I found that there are definite trends in certain areas for particular designs. Most importantly, that the hand of the individual knitter can be seen quite clearly in the small seeding sections, the choice of larger motifs and the way the garment has been constructed. This has been distilled sometimes by the knitter finding a magazine pattern or indeed having seen Gladys Thompson's book, but overall, there is something of the place and of the family that shines through.

The Cornish designs in general tend towards horizontal patterning with a lot of texture created in the fabric of the knit. The use of the simple basketweave, for example, can distort the knitting to give a far more complex look than the actual knitting needed to be. It reflects the surface of the sea and as in the musician's pattern (see *Pattern Directory: Herringbones, Polperro, Cornwall*) it is really quite lyrical. The East Neuk and Scottish Fleet Ganseys tend towards vertical patterning with recurring features of flags, hearts, diamonds etc. The northern Scottish designs have far more complex seeding sections

happening with intricate larger motifs such as the anchor pattern. Some of the most complex and densely patterned garments were from the far north of Scotland but there is evidence that they have been adapted and used further down the coast, as far as Filey, in North Yorkshire. This has been well documented in the past, with knitters from Filey noting that their ideas came from the north. The biggest influence on the flow of design knowledge around the coast of the UK was herring fishing and it undoubtedly created a huge movement of folk and the subsequent sharing of ideas.

Eriskay Ganseys are of particular interest: Eriskay is part of the Western Isles or Outer Hebrides.

The first Hebridean Gansey I saw was from Barra, the southern-most island, and was in Gladys Thompson's book. When I lived on Skye, I became aware of the knitting co-operative on the isle of Eriskay, set up by the local parish priest. Many of these cream Ganseys were knitted for sale and are amazingly decorative with lace patterns and unusual motifs, including the 'Starfish' and the 'Print O'the Hoof' patterns, both of which I have used in the projects for this book (see *Projects: The Calypso Summer Vest* and *Cardium Gansey Shawl*).

Michael Pearson' excellent book *Traditional Knitting: Aran, Fair Isle and Fisher Ganseys* has a large section dedicated to these Eriskay Ganseys. Knitting these was a way to add to a family's income in a crofting community where everyone had several jobs on the go at once. A bit of knitting, fishing, collecting winkles etc, something I was very familiar with, having spent years doing the same in my youth.

The economic necessity of hand knitting for some communities has lasted well beyond the rest of the country. In the Western Isles, Shetland and the north of Scotland knitting in the twentieth century continued with supplying Aran sweaters for the Aran Isles and Dublin stores, Fair Isle yoked garments for the fashion trade from the early 1900s and lace, which was encouraged in Shetland as an enterprise. These inventive knitters were very good at adapting patterns and, looking at the 'Star' designs of the Hebrides, one can easily see the resemblance in stitch patterning to the colourwork of Fair Isle stranded designs. We noticed in many Ganseys from the north how Aran stitches had crept into some of the traditional knits... travelling cables for example.

*Isabella's son aboard the Kiloran,
skippered by Campbell Thomson*

Ganseys through time

Sheila and I spent many hours examining the Ganseys in this book and at the Scottish Fisheries Museum. We discovered how one knitter, Robina, had experimented in the sleeve decreasing for her first Gansey, where she had used k2tog in a variety of places apart from down the neat seam stitch. On the second sleeve she had improved and by her second Gansey the decreases were perfect. She was obviously trying to achieve a perfect fit for her fisherman son Tam. A word about Tam Easson, who volunteered at the Museum, from Jen Gordon, who is a textile expert and curator, and wrote a beautiful piece about this amazing man. His own Gansey, knitted in cream by his mother Robina, was one we admired in the collection.

Jen wrote: "Tam Easson left school at the age of 14 to go 'cooking' aboard the fishing boat Violet. At the age of 20, on the outbreak of World War II, he joined the crew of the Naval ship Solena, and spent the next seven years patrolling the Arctic Circle. He swiftly rose to the rank of petty officer, which involved bookkeeping and 'keeping the peace' on board. Experienced fishermen were employed on trawlers and drifters in minesweeping and boom defence duties, but apprentice seamen and landlubbers were employed in what Tam said was known as 'Harry Tate's Navy'! Jen always remembers him in his beautiful Gansey.

We also saw how one particular knitter tried out a diamond pattern on her first round and thereafter adjusted the second diamond rounds, obviously unhappy with the first but not prepared to take it out. The mends were breathtaking and showed the love and mindfulness necessary to maintain the garment so it could even be passed on to another generation. There were lots of techniques used to extend the life of a Gansey: sometimes the cuffs were simply cut off and knitted back down in a newer, brighter yarn, and occasionally this happened several times so that the age of the garment was reflected in different yarns used in the re-knitting. We saw pristine Ganseys made for sale that had been put away in storage and garments so well worn that the patterning was disappearing into the fabric of the knit at the wear spots. Remarkably, there are also examples of Ganseys ninety to a hundred years old, which could be worn again today with a little love and attention.

White hand-knitted gansey with cables and moss stitch diamond pattern. Knitted by Robina Jack for her son, for when he left Cellardyke to serve in the Royal Navy, at the outbreak of the Second World War. Scottish Fisheries Museum Collection, ANSFM:2007.9

Traditional Ganseys in splendid colours from the collection at the Scottish Fisheries Museum. Photo by Di Gilpin

Lace tree of life, horseshoes and diamonds, with star, anchor, tree of life, diamond and cables, Eriskay.
Scottish Fisheries Museum Collection, ANSFM:2019.398

A subtle change in wool shows the repair in this sleeve in the Scottish Fisheries Museum Collection, ANSFM:1994.209.4. Photo by Di Gilpin

Repairs to one of Anji's grandfather's Ganseys, a well-worn and well-loved garment!

TOOLS AND MATERIALS

YARN

Traditionally Ganseys were knitted in a 5ply worsted-spun wool. We have used a traditional yarn for our *Hudson Sleeveless Slip Over* (see *Projects*). Many different yarns are suitable for Gansey knitting. In our research we found that Gansey knitters also used a variety of DK weight yarns, some with a blend of colour in the Scottish way. To allow for pattern visibility we would not recommend a yarn with a loft or with a very pronounced marl or variegated effect. We created our Lalland DK as a 4ply with 2x2 twists and then a final twist in the spinning - this allows for proper stitch definition. Gansey projects would also look great in cotton and linen yarns, as in our summer vest *The Calypso* (see *Projects*). Don't feel constrained to use one particular kind of yarn, just make sure to swatch and check your tension (gauge). It may be that it's better to go down a needle size than recommended for the yarn you choose.

All of the Pattern Directory samples are knitted in our Lalland DK, from a selection of gorgeous shades such as Crowdie, Haar, Linnet and Sea Purslane

NEEDLES

For our modern patterns (see *Projects*), we specify using the traditional set of 5 long double-pointed needles where possible. These can be replaced with circular needles, worked in the round with stitch markers, but the tension (gauge) has to be regularly checked as it is more difficult to create that tension and stitch definition using a circular needle. We would also recommend trying a knitting belt with the double-pointed needles, as seen in the wonderful photograph of Isabella with her 'whisker and wires' (see *A Short History of Ganseys: Isabella Stewart - Gansey knitter and 'herring quine'*).

My knitting belt, originally ordered by letter from Shetland when I was living in the Isle of Skye. While I made up my own way of using it, there are now plenty of tutorials online, so why not give it a try yourself!

OTHER SUPPLIES

Good lighting is essential for knitting in the round, especially if you are using a darker colour yarn.

This book is designed for you to pick and choose your own favourite motifs to add into several of the patterns. For example, with our *Sea Biscuit Cardigan* (see *Projects*), there are a variety of diamonds or hearts you could add into the design to make it your own!

If you would like to chart your own designs or motifs, it is now possible to print off your own graph paper from a variety of knitting graph paper websites. These can be made to your own particular tension, which is really helpful. To complete a Gansey project, you will of course also need

Graph paper can make each project your own

your favourite knitting accessories, such as a darning (tapestry) needle for sewing up, a cable needle, needle stoppers (point protectors), waste yarn/stitch holders, scissors, measuring tape, spare short double-pointed needles for grafting, stitch markers, row/round counters, pen and paper to mark off progress on a chart and perhaps a steam iron for blocking.

Some of our favourite knitting tools

GANSEY TECHNIQUES AND CONSTRUCTION

Ganseys are constructed in specific ways. Most of these have evolved to create a hard-wearing garment.

One of the defining features is the underarm gusset, necessary for such a tight-fitting garment. After half the underarm gusset has been worked, the front and back of the body are then knitted separately, on two needles to the shoulders. The shoulders may be joined with a 3-needle cast off, grafted or even joined using a shoulder strap or shoulder saddle.

Once the front and back parts are joined at the shoulder, stitches are picked up round the armhole, including the underarm gusset stitches from the holder, and the sleeve is knitted down to the cuff in the round. This allows a frayed Gansey cuff to be re-knitted easily by cutting off the cuff, picking up the stitches and knitting down. Alternatively, the wool could be unravelled from the cuff upwards, to allow repair of the lower sleeve when it became too worn.

Traditionally Gansey sleeves are shorter to avoid the cuffs catching as the fishermen work. The neck band can be completed in a variety of different ways, often with a neck gusset added to ensure the Gansey neck does not chafe the wearer.

GUSSETS

Gussets are a wonderful device used in Gansey knitting that add extra ease at the underarm of the garment. In the traditional Gansey this was a utilitarian feature, included to allow the fisherman increased freedom of movement as he worked on the boat.

The underarm gusset begins with the 'false seam', which runs up from the welt, and can be made up of one or several stitches. Because Ganseys are knitted in the round, the false seam is also a lovely way of marking your place within the knitting.

The knitter can either begin to increase for the gusset into the central seam stitch itself, or in the stitches at either side of the false seam. After the gusset increases are complete, the stitches are put on hold while the upper body is worked. Once the shoulders have been joined, stitches are picked up around the arm opening for the sleeves and the gusset stitches are worked again, this time being decreased away as the sleeve is worked downwards.

Through our research we found examples of gussets decorated to either side with cables or seed stitches, which were then repeated in the all-over pattern in the garment. This photograph features a wonderful Gansey from the Scottish Fisheries Museum, where you can see the very special Tree of Life design either side of the gusset. The gusset itself begins with a false seam of seed stitches that at first glance resemble a cable pattern. This mock cable seeding is repeated in columns at the outer edges of the Tree of Life patterning.

Knitters sometimes modified the shape of the gusset to fine tune the size of the sleeves and the body at the chest. This allowed for more ease in the Gansey when worn; very helpful in garments that were dense, and knitted at incredibly tight tension (gauge). However, gussets generally work best as very regular diamond symmetrical inserts with even rates of increasing (in the body) and decreasing (in the sleeves). We have found some very individual versions during our research at the Scottish Fisheries Museum.

Gusset with Tree of Life borders. Scottish Fisheries Museum Collection, ANSFM:1994.209.7. Photo by Di Gilpin

WORKING A SAMPLE UNDERARM GUSSET

The simple gusset is a stocking (stockinette) stitch diamond gusset bordered by reverse stocking (reverse stockinette) stitch leading from a false seam of two purl stitches. It is a very pleasing and neat gusset and a useful tool in all sorts of ways (see *Other uses for gussets*).

The other gusset samples are variations from the simple gusset.

We recommend knitting each gusset as shown on the chart to practise the increasing and decreasing particular to gusset knitting. In the sample we have increased and decreased on every fourth row but this can be adjusted when incorporating a gusset into a pattern or garment.

Simple gusset

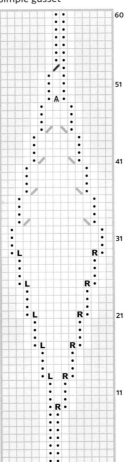

Centre seam stitch gusset

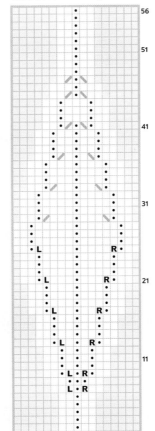

Gusset with cable edges

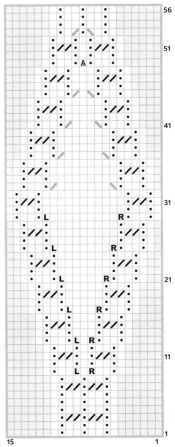

KEY

☐ RS: knit WS: purl	**L** M1L	◣ skp	**A** sk2p	⁄⁄ Cable 2 Right
• RS: purl WS: knit	**R** M1R	⁄ k2tog	⁄ p2tog	☐ no stitch

WORKING RIGHT- AND LEFT-LEANING INCREASES IN THE GUSSET

The illustrations below show a right-leaning increase (M1R), which always occurs first and nearest the right-hand edge of your knitting, and a left-leaning increase (M1L), which is made after the gusset stitches have been worked across.

M1R (MAKE A RIGHT-LEANING INCREASE)

Step one: Pick up the loop between stitches from back to front

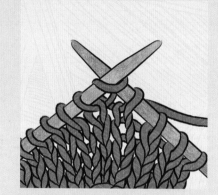

Step two: Knit into the front of the picked-up loop to create the new stitch

M1L (MAKE A LEFT-LEANING INCREASE)

Step one: Pick up the loop between stitches from front to back

Step two: Knit into the back of the picked-up loop to create the new stitch

WORKING RIGHT- AND LEFT-LEANING DECREASES IN THE GUSSET

The illustrations below show a left-leaning decrease (skp), which always occurs first and nearest the right-hand edge of your knitting, and a right-leaning decrease (k2tog), which is made after the gusset stitches have been worked across.

SKP (LEFT-LEANING DECREASE)

Step one: Insert the right needle knitwise into the first stitch on the left needle

Step two: Slip the stitch to the right needle without knitting it

Step three: Knit the next stitch on the left needle as normal

Step four: Insert the left needle from left to right into the second stitch on the right needle

Step five: Pull the second stitch over the first stitch and off the right needle to decrease one stitch

K2TOG (RIGHT-LEANING DECREASE)

Step one: Insert right needle knitwise into first two stitches on left needle, as if to knit

Step two: Wrap yarn around right needle as usual

Step three: Pull yarn through these stitches

Step four: Pull stitches off left needle to decrease one stitch

GANSEY NECK GUSSETS

Gansey neck gussets are a great device for the traditional slash neck as they allow the collar, knitted at the end, to be wider and to sit out away from the neck. They were used in Ganseys when there was no saddle or shoulder strap (see below), so the wearer did not have to endure a chafed neck exacerbated by the salt water and fish scales! The neck gussets push the collar outwards, and the wearer could then fit a 'neckerchief' or small scarf inside the collar.

To make the gusset, work 3-needle cast (bind) off (see *General Techniques*) of the number of stitches needed for the shoulder, less the number of stitches being taken into the gusset, leaving the remainder of the sts for the other shoulder and neck on two needles. Starting from the last stitch of the cast (bind) off, use a third needle to pick up the last stitch from the cast-off (bound-off) section and knit it, then knit the stitch on the first needle, turn and p2, then purl a stitch from the second needle. Turn and k3, then knit a stitch from the first side. Repeat across the rows using stocking (stockinette) stitch until you have incorporated the total number of stitches you would like into the gusset on both sides.

Leave on a stitch holder while you repeat for the other neck gusset. Put all the stitches including the central stitches back and front of the collar onto a set of four short double-pointed needles and continue with the collar.

Neck gussets would be used instead of a saddle or shoulder strap

OTHER USES FOR GUSSETS

We have used the short gusset for gloves below in the *Caledonia Fingerless Gloves* design (see *Projects*) to show how versatile gussets can be when making other items.

The short gusset for gloves has a three-stitch false seam, made up of (p1, k1, p1). Increases are made either side of the central knitted seam stitch. This means you don't have to create a central knit seam stitch

to allow for the increases; it is already there!

We further explore the gusset as a device in the beautiful *Cardium Gansey Shawl* design (see *Projects*) featuring the Print O' the Hoof stitch pattern, which we have identified in many Eriskay Ganseys from the Western Isles of Scotland.

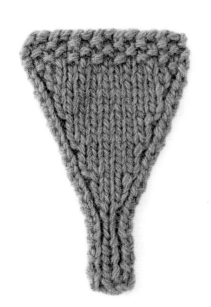

Gusset sample worked according to the chart for the *Caledonia Fingerless Gloves*

KEY

	RS: knit WS: purl	**L** M1L
•	RS: purl WS: knit	**R** M1R

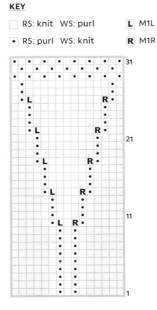

Short gusset for gloves

Thumb gussets use increases for shaping

GANSEY TECHNIQUES AND CONSTRUCTION

SHOULDER STRAPS

Throughout all coastal areas from Cornwall to Caithness, the most widely-used shoulder strap, or extension, is the 'rig and furrow'. 'Rig and furrow' describes the earliest form of organised agriculture and the system seen throughout the UK and particularly in Scotland. The rig was built up with organic material to increase fertility and in the Western Isles the use of seaweed was frequent, particularly for the cultivation of the potato.

I was fortunate enough to sail a lot in my youth around these islands, one of the finest ways to view the incredible mountains of Harris, Rhum and Skye. On a windy day of sun and cloud, the lines of the rigs and the hollows of the furrows appear as if by magic in the landscape, creating linear patterns on the hillsides, now de-populated from the terrible clearances of the 18th and 19th centuries, overgrown and unproductive, yet clearly visible as a reminder of hundreds of years of agriculture in these remote places.

To make the shoulder strap, the shoulder stitches are knitted up from the front yoke in alternating bands, usually 3 rows of reverse stocking (reverse stockinette) stitch, followed by 2 rows of stocking (stockinette) stitch, over 28 or 33 rows, ending with 3 rows of reverse stocking stitch.

This is then joined on to the back shoulder, either by an internal 3-needle cast (bind) off or by grafting. We did examine a Gansey where the straps were made with one worked from the front to the back and the other worked from the back to the front... both then grafted. Another sign of the individual nature of each garment and the hand of the knitter who made it.

THE ERISKAY SHOULDER STRAP

The Eriskay shoulder strap consists of favourite pattern elements, usually including a diamond trellis with bands of decorative horizontal slipped stitches or garter slip stitches, and is found in many of the Ganseys knitted by Cath McMillan for the Eriskay Co-operative that started in the 1970s. These slip stitches are referred to elsewhere as 'corn stitches', with possible reference to the 'stooks' of barley or wheat from scything the crop. It is almost a form of lace and does require firm handling. We have noticed it has the same elements as the mock cables of Mrs Elsie Buchan of Peterhead on the mainland; a slipped stitch and a yarn forward. The similarities end there, however, in the way the stitches behave and are indicative of these two clever and inventive knitters.

Eriskay Shoulder Strap with diamonds and corn stitches

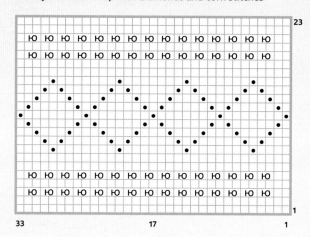

KEY

☐ RS: knit   WS: purl

⊡ RS: purl   WS: knit

Ю corn stitch

Eriskay shoulder strap, ready to graft

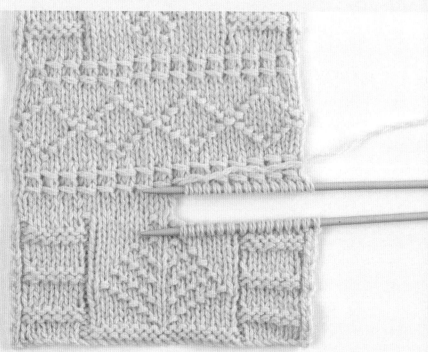

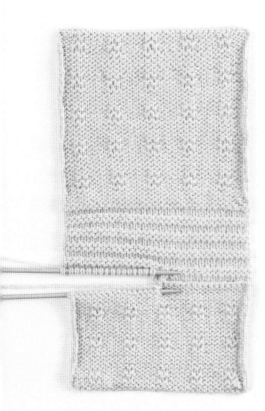

Rig and Furrow
shoulder strap,
worked from
wrong side

Half way through internal 3-needle cast
(bind) off on Rig and Furrow shoulder
strap, showing the right side

SHOULDER SADDLES

The shoulder saddle is a much more
complex construction than the shoulder
strap. The saddle - always featuring a
pattern from the yoke, such as zigzags or
chevrons - is created from a provisional
cast on for the required number of stitches
plus 2 stitches for the edges. The centre
band is then joined to each set of shoulder
stitches as follows:

Row 1 (WS): Slip 1 purlwise, pattern to last
stitch, work a p2tog with the last stitch of
the band and the next stitch from the yoke.

Row 2 (RS): Slip 1 purlwise, pattern to last
stitch, work a skp with the last stitch of the
band and the next stitch from the yoke.

The edge stitches must be kept very tight
and neat, and it will usually be necessary
to take 2 stitches from each yoke every
few rows, to ensure a flat shoulder. This
is because you will have more stitches
than rows in your tension (gauge). This is a
complex but satisfying way of working the
shoulder join, enabling the saddle pattern
to be carried on down the centre sleeve
and the stitches from the provisional cast
on to be used in the neck band.

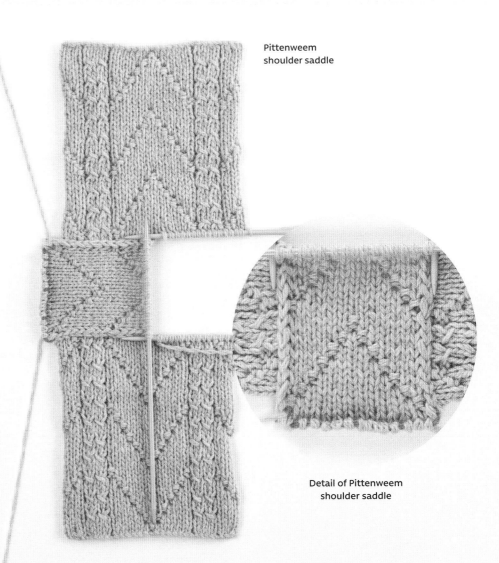

Pittenweem
shoulder saddle

Detail of Pittenweem
shoulder saddle

PATTERN DIRECTORY

FOULA.
SHETLAND

THE MINCH

WICK
BUCKIE
FORRES
WHITEHILLS
HOPEMAN
BANFF
ROSEMARKIE
FRASERBURGH
AVOCH
INVERALLOCHY
ISLE OF
SKYE
NAIRN
INVERNESS
PETERHEAD
ERISKAY
CRUDEN BAY
BARRA
MALLAIG
ARBROATH
FIFE
EAST NEUK
KIRKCALDY
ANSTRUTHER
LEITH
PITTENWEEM
MUSSELBURGH
SEAHOUSES
AMBLE
NEWBIGGIN
NORTHUMBERLAND
YORKSHIRE
SCARBOROUGH
FLAMBOROUGH
FILEY
HUMBER RIVER
SHERINGHAM
NORFOLK
GREAT
YARMOUTH
MORWENSTOW
BUDE
CORNWALL
ST.IVES
LOOE. EDDYSTONE
LIGHTHOUSE
SENNEN
POLPERRO
THE
LIZARD

DIAMONDS

THEIR SYMMETRY IS SPECTACULAR

Diamond patterns in Gansey knitting are numerous and very varied. Loved by knitters, they appear in many, many forms and show up in villages and collections all around the British coast. Some particular ones are specific to a place and others occur almost everywhere. Their symmetry is spectacular and allows them to fit any size of panel, which makes them a great device for knitters working out the numbers in their Gansey designs. They occur individually, in pairs and as a knitted 'fabric' as in the Inverallochy Diamonds pattern.

In our research we found as yet only one that starts with two purl stitches and continues as an even number pattern (see *Diamonds with a Difference*). The rest are all worked over an odd number of stitches, centring round a single purl stitch as the starting point. Knitters have used moss stitch, double moss, stocking (stockinette) stitch and more to fill in the diamond shape, so the variety is enormous. The stitch definition is tremendous in this form of pattern and works beautifully as a single motif in horizontal bands, but also as vertical lines of diamonds, for example in the Gansey knitted by Mrs Edwards of Inverallochy, on the north east Scottish coast, referenced by Michael Pearson in his book *Traditional Knitting*. Pearson also notes that the diamond design predominantly came from Scotland and quotes Mrs Noble from Filey: "...the moss and the diamond came from the Scottish when they came for the herring, they used to knit on eight short needles - they taught me the anchor and the chevron and they did a plait instead of a cable. There was another one from Scotland - the half flag - me mother used to do that one without ropes. The ladder was more traditional for Filey and not the diamond."

It seems patterns travelled the coast and particularly with the herring girls. Starting from the northern and western areas of Scotland they moved south and the special themes and motifs travelled with them. There are many names ascribed to the diamond designs from 'fishing nets' to 'church windows'; the latter seems very appropriate for designs from the East Neuk in Fife, where each village had landmark churches in prominent positions to help guide fishermen on their boats safely home.

SMALL SINGLE DIAMONDS

KEY

☐ RS: knit   WS: purl

• RS: purl   WS: knit

Fraserburgh, Aberdeenshire 1

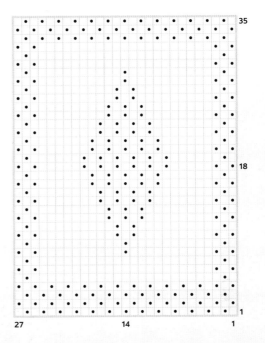

Fraserburgh, Aberdeenshire 2

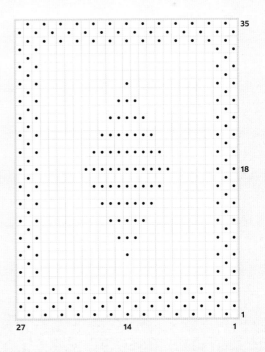

DIAMOND PATTERNS

Inverallochy, Aberdeenshire

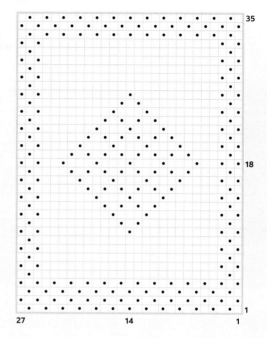

Cruden Bay, Aberdeenshire

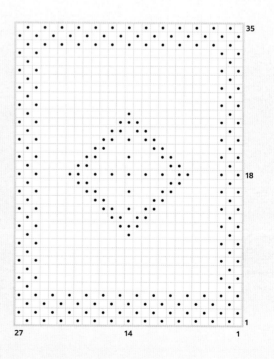

KEY

☐ RS: knit   WS: purl

• RS: purl   WS: knit

Buckie, Aberdeenshire

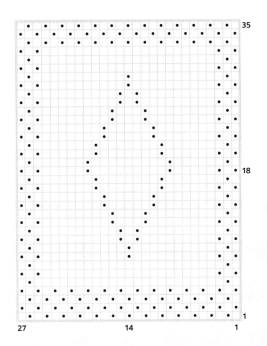

Scottish Fleet

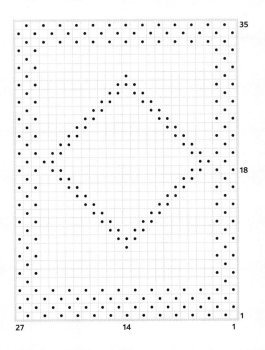

Mallaig, West Highlands

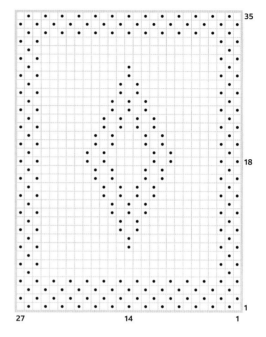

Eriskay, Western Isles

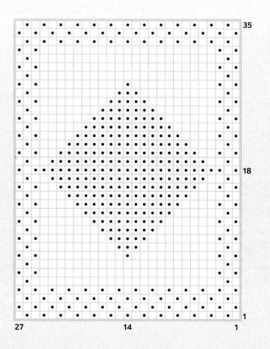

SMALL DOUBLE DIAMONDS

KEY

☐ RS: knit   WS: purl

• RS: purl   WS: knit

Buckie, Aberdeenshire

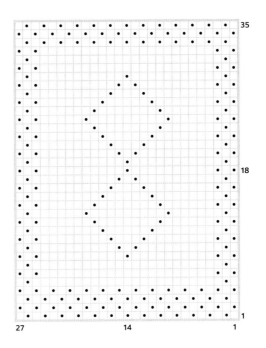

Banff, Aberdeenshire

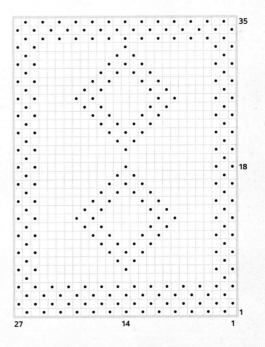

East Neuk, Fife

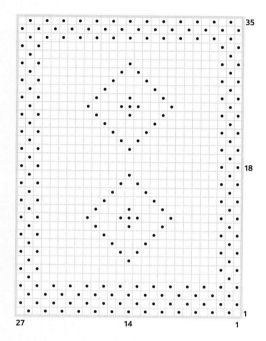

Leith, Edinburgh

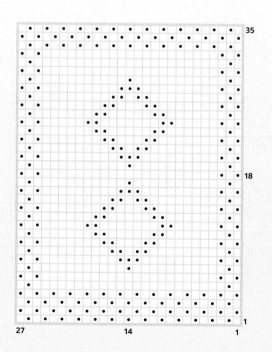

Amble, Northumberland

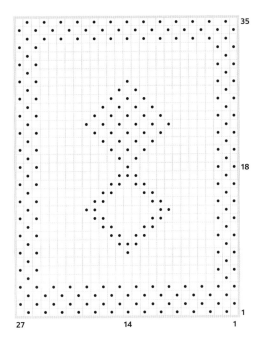

Buckie, Aberdeenshire

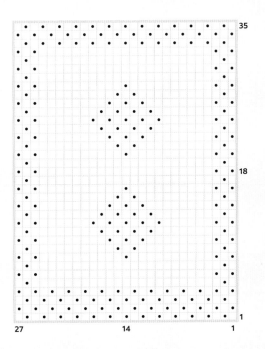

Peterhead, Aberdeenshire

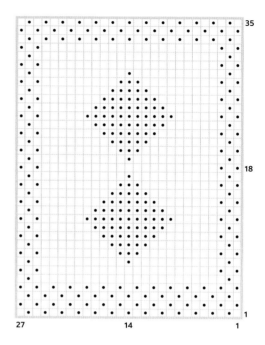

Inverness, Highlands

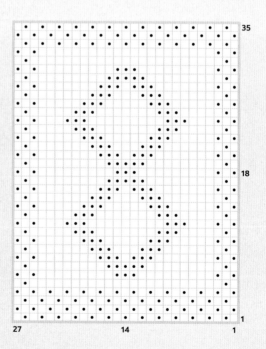

SMALL DIAMOND PROGRESSIONS

KEY

☐ RS: knit   WS: purl

• RS: purl   WS: knit

Rosemarkie, Aberdeenshire

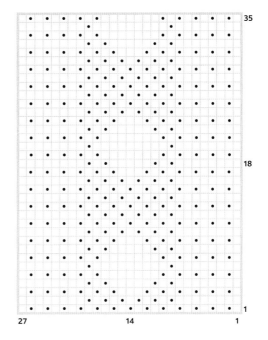

Inverallochy, Aberdeenshire

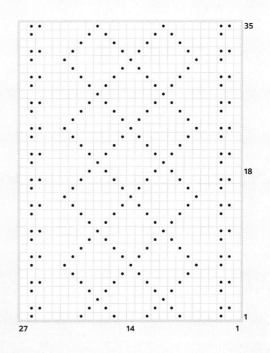

LARGE DIAMONDS

Eriskay, Western Isles

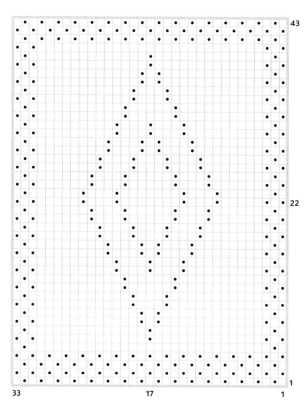

Humber River, Northern England

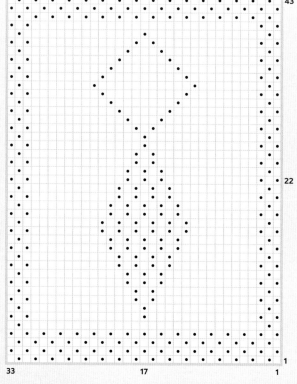

Kirkcaldy, Fife

KEY

☐ RS: knit   WS: purl

• RS: purl   WS: knit

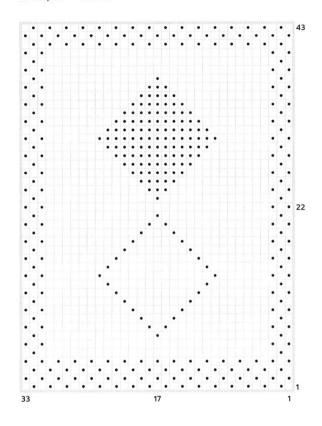

Musselburgh, East Lothian

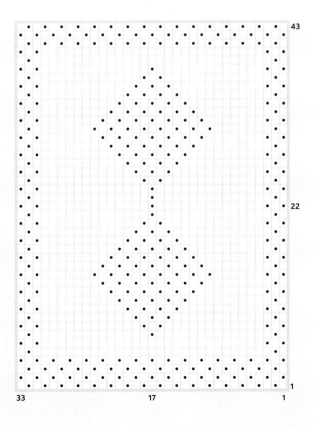

43

Foula, Shetland

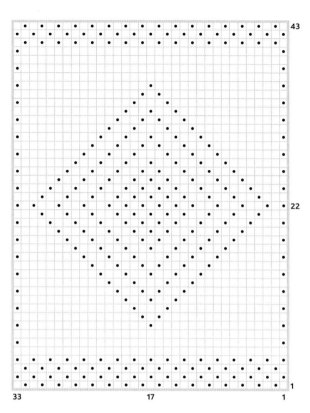

Nairn, Moray Firth

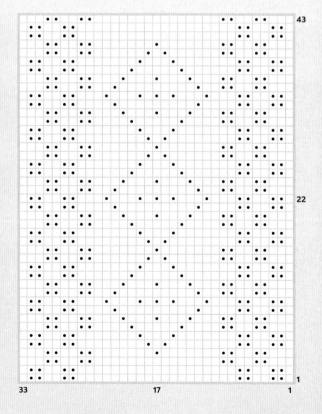

KEY

☐ RS: knit   WS: purl

• RS: purl   WS: knit

Polperro, Cornwall

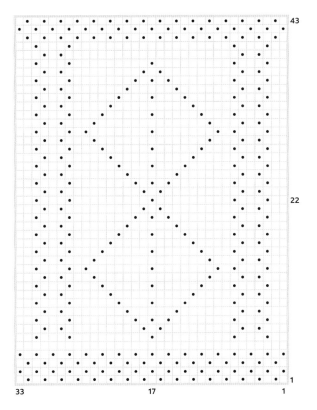

Flamborough, Yorkshire

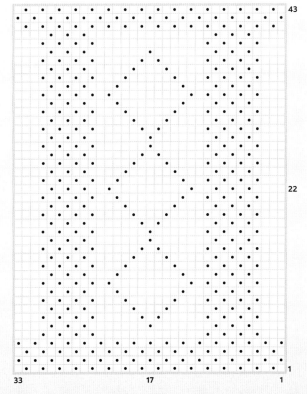

DIAMONDS WITH A DIFFERENCE

There are many, many diamond designs and
variations but two stand out. The first is the
Sheringham diamond with herringbone. Most
importantly, it is just about the only diamond
created with even numbers. It starts with a set
of two by two purl stitches, that are beautifully
recreated at the apex of the herringbone/
chevron too. As a 2-stitch diamond it looks quite
different, more defined and detailed and stands
alone in its evenness.

The Fraserburgh diamonds are open diamonds
and created by the tremendous knitter, Mrs Elsie
Buchan. They are so clever and intricate, never
quite closing and with, classic for Elsie, a double
mock cable seeding pattern running down the
centre of one of the diamond shapes to give
texture and depth to the patterning. Such a neat
combination of elements shows the true level of
creativity in these knitters. We love Elsie!

Sheringham, Norfolk

KEY

☐	RS: knit WS: purl
⊡	RS: purl WS: knit
ℕ	Mock Cable

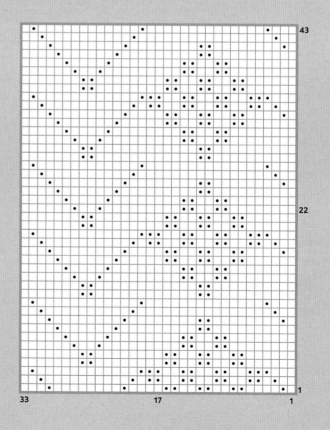

Fraserburgh, Aberdeenshire

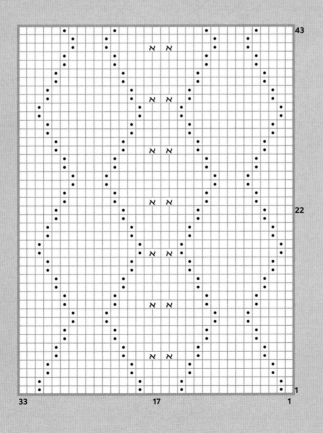

CABLES

DRAMATIC AND DISTINCTIVE

There are a great many fabulous cable patterns, from Scotland and Cornwall in particular. Representing ropes or the ship's rigging, the cables are dramatic and used to great effect. Apart from the seeding two-stitch cables, the smallest main cables predominate along the eastern shores of England. They are very regulated and with little variation, as seen in the Filey, Yorkshire, sample, which may well have been inspired by the Wick, Caithness, double cable with mini ladders running up the sides.

Of particular note are the Cornish cables. In Polperro the snake cable with ladders is well-recorded and in a class of its own! The very special St Ives sample, like many Cornish patterns explored in this book, creates a fabric in itself, with moving cables looking like the wild seas off the Lizard Point at the southern tip of the country.

Scottish cables are equally distinctive. The Inverness cable is combined with flag/triangle designs and in Avoch there are crab claw cables. My favourite from Forres, used in our sock design, is of cabling on an open bed of stocking (stockinette) stitch, with ladders worked as seeding stitches between. Again, this creates more of a 'fabric' rather than a strictly vertical-patterned section.

Sheila noted many years ago that these cables can often cause a distortion to the overall patterning on a Gansey, as the tension (gauge) changes so much with the crossing of the stitches. This causes a droop or a wavy line effect unless corrected by the addition of extra stitches at the start of the cabling, which are removed at the end.

All of the beautiful cable samples Sheila has knitted have fewer stitches at the cast-on and cast-off (bound-off) edges than are needed for the actual cables, with extra stitches added into the cables immediately before the first cable row, and then decreased immediately after the final cable row to keep the edges flat, but we have generally not shown this in the charts. For example, for a 12-stitch cable, only 8 stitches would be cast on, and then 4 extra stitches added in while the cable is worked.

SMALL CABLES

Filey, Yorkshire

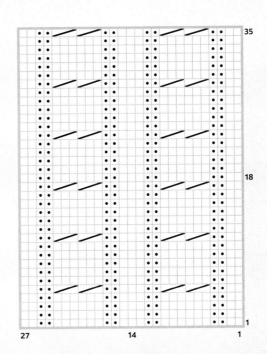

KEY

☐ RS: knit	WS: purl
▪ RS: purl	WS: knit
╱╱╱	Cable 6 Right

Wick, Caithness

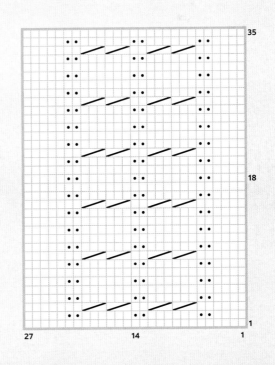

Bude, Cornwall

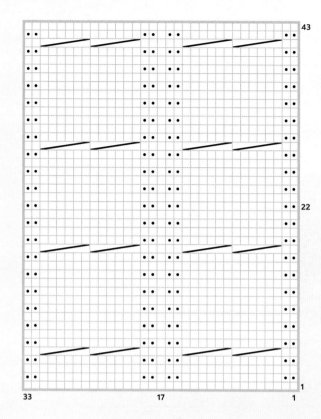

Avoch, Aberdeenshire

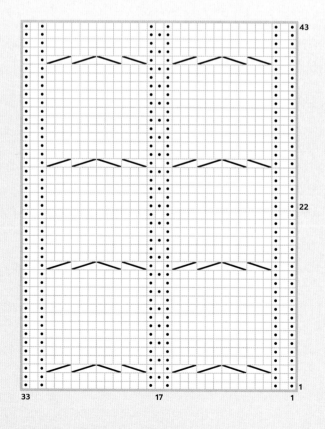

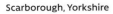

Scarborough, Yorkshire

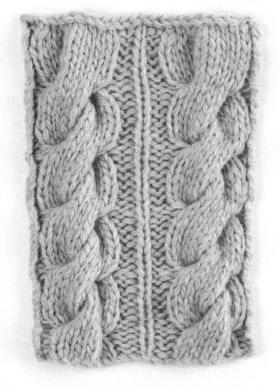

KEY

☐ RS: knit WS: purl	
• RS: purl WS: knit	

Cable 6 Right

Cable 6 Left

Cable 12 Right

Inverness, Highlands

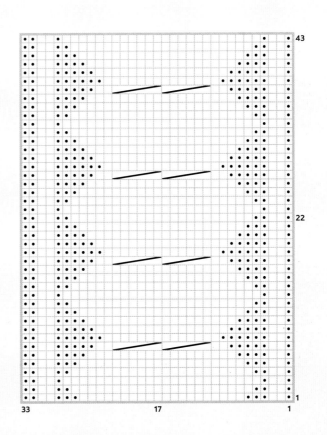

51

CABLE PATTERNS

Polperro, Cornwall

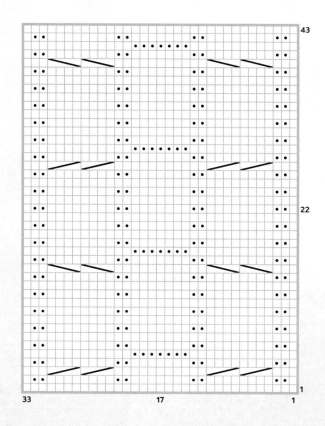

St Ives, Cornwall

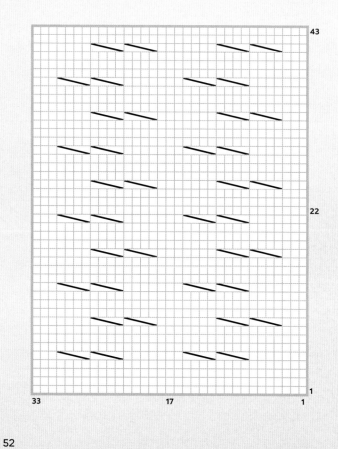

RS: knit   WS: purl   Cable 8 Left

• RS: purl   WS: knit   Cable 8 Right

Sennen Cove, Cornwall

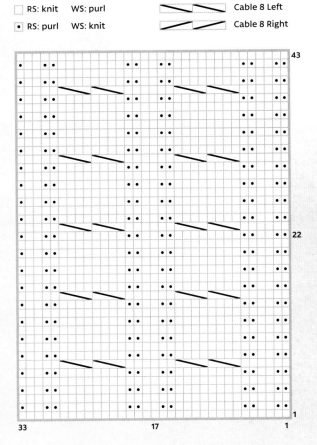

Forres, Aberdeenshire

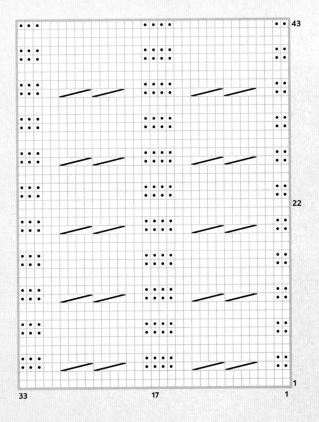

CABLE PATTERNS

CABLE PROGRESSIONS

KEY

☐ RS: knit	WS: purl	Cable 4 Left
• RS: purl	WS: knit	Cable 6 Right

English Coast

B   A

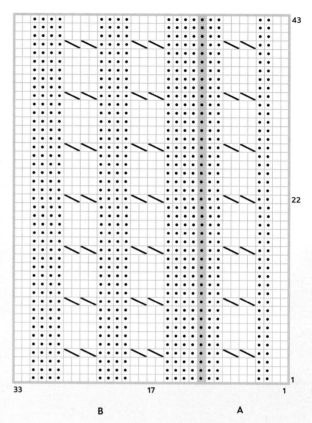

33   17   1

B   A

Scottish Fleet

B   A

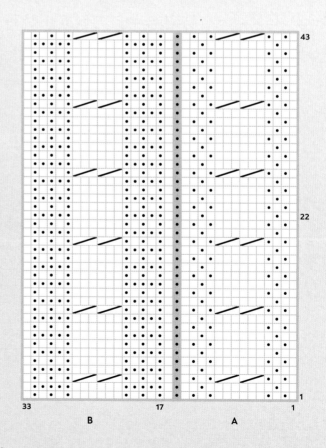

33   17   1

B   A

PITTENWEEM BASKETWEAVE AND CABLE

This is a truly intriguing pattern that we both feel is incredibly special. We found the Gansey in the East Neuk Collection at the Scottish Fisheries Museum as part of our recording work there. We both let out a gasp, which has happened throughout this journey, but not that often. Here is a fascinating combination of two popular Gansey patterns. A basic 8-stitch/16-round pattern is transformed by creating a 2-stitch cable up the centre of the purl segments. This is done by increasing in the first round of the purl segment, to create 2 extra stitches, then twisting the 2 centre stitches on every round, before decreasing twice again at the start of the following knit section. This pattern repeat is begun over 8 stitches, but increases to 10 stitches on the foundation (set-up) round. When all repeats of the pattern are complete the pattern can be decreased to 8 stitches again on the final round. The repeat is 16 rounds long, so the initial increase round, and the final repeat with its ending decreases should be taken into account when planning to use this stitch pattern.

Pittenweem Basketweave and Cable

BENEFITS OF WORKING IN THE ROUND

Sheila notes that this pattern is much easier to work in the round than back and forth (see *Projects: Findhorn Gansey Boot Socks* for how we use this as an option for the cuff).

Working in the round, the pattern would be as follows:

(over 8 sts and 16 rounds repeat)

Foundation round: P4, k4.

Round 2: K4, p1, M1L, p2, M1L, p1.

Rounds 3-9: K4, p2, Cable 2 Right, p2.

Round 10: P1, M1L, p2, M1L, p1, k1, k2tog, k2tog, k1.

Rounds 11-17: P2, Cable 2 right, p2, k4.

Repeat rounds 2-17.

Finishing round (round 34): K1, k2tog, k2tog, k1, k4.

Note that you'll work the foundation and finishing rounds only once to start and complete the pattern.

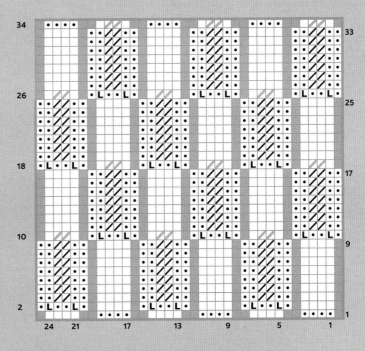

KEY

☐ RS: knit WS: purl		⧫ Cable 2 Left
• RS: purl WS: knit		⧄ RS: k2tog WS: p2tog
▨ No stitch		L M1L

TREE OF LIFE

SYMBOLIC ACROSS CULTURES

We have found some fabulous Tree of Life designs in our search in Scotland. From tiny wee trees to some magnificent, many-branched versions and, in particular, from the collection at the Anstruther Fisheries Museum. The Tree of Life is symbolic across many faiths and cultures and falls into a special category of motifs in Gansey knitting. Mostly found in Scottish Ganseys, we particularly love the Anstruther Tree, which also looks remarkably like the bones of a herring! Maybe a pun by the knitter? I have taken it as such and use it in one of our garments *The Calypso Summer Vest* (see *Projects*).

One of the large tree patterns in this section is an amazing Tree of Life design, attributed to Mrs Laidlaw of Seahouses, Northumberland, and highlighted by Gladys Thompson, and was flanked with vertical rows of flags but is just as wonderful on its own.

SMALL TREES

KEY

☐ RS: knit   WS: purl

• RS: purl   WS: knit

Boddam, Peterhead

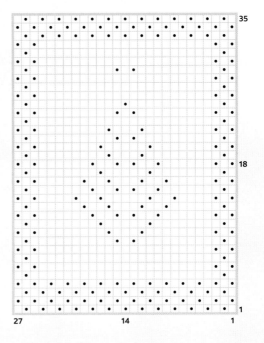

Peterhead, Aberdeenshire

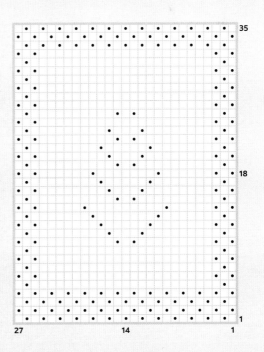

Fraserburgh, Aberdeenshire

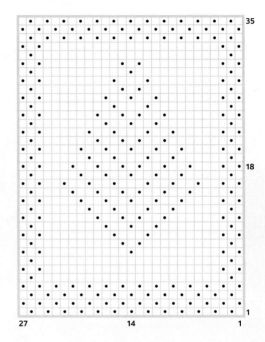

Scottish Coast

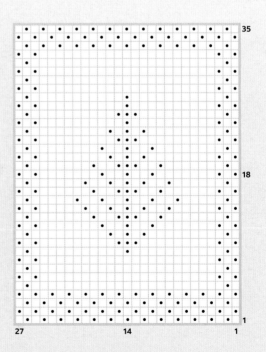

LARGE TREES

Eriskay, Western Isles

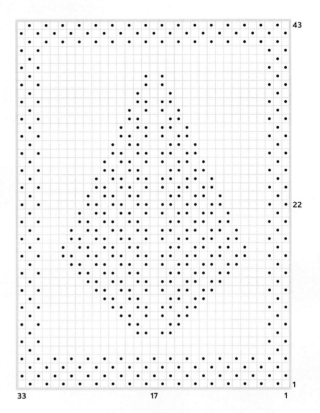

Peterhead, Aberdeenshire

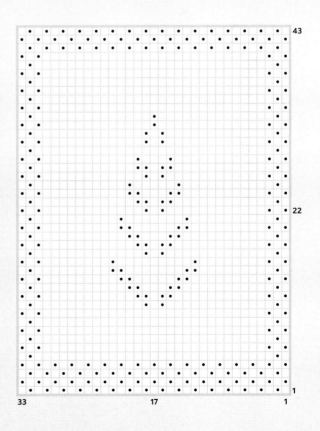

59

Seahouses, Northumberland

KEY

☐ RS: knit WS: purl

• RS: purl WS: knit

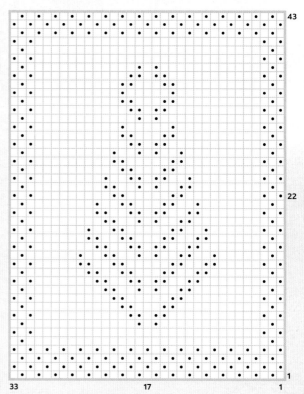

Anstruther, Fife

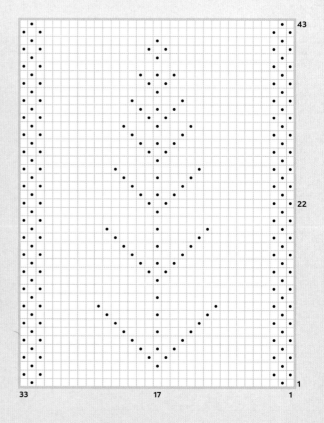

ERISKAY, WESTERN ISLES, TREE OF LIFE

Gladys Thompson mentions and shows a beautiful Gansey from the Isle of Barra, close to Eriskay, in her book *Patterns for Guernseys, Jerseys & Arans* (Dover, 2000). This may have inspired the co-operative created in the 1970s on the island of Eriskay, which had a group of hand knitters within its core. The Ganseys made by the co-operative are quite incredible and in fact almost not Ganseys at all, as they have lace patterns happily sitting next to classic cables, diamonds and more. I have asked myself so many times, "Would any self-respecting fisherman go to sea wearing lace?" The answer is clear to me. No! These Ganseys were made as 'Sunday Best' or even to be married in, and also to be sold.

There are some incredible and adventurous knitters in this co-op and sadly I have been unable to chat to any of them so many years later, although I knew of them when I lived across the water in Skye. I have so many questions about the use of lace designs. Did they come from knowledge of Shetland lace? Also, the cables, sometimes travelling, normally only appear in Aran knitting. The knowledge that many women in the Western Isles were contract knitting for the Aran stores in Ireland for more than a hundred years, also gives me pause for thought.

There are so many different influences in these pieces and so many symbolic designs used, that it is hard to decipher them and establish a clear origin, except to say that some of these are legendary, as the sample here of the Tree of Life in lace, with great seeding stitches and framed with the wonderful 'corn stitch' or horizontal seed stitch, which also acts as a wee line of lace too. I could not resist using an Eriskay lace Print O' the Hoof design for our *Cardium Gansey Shawl* (see *Projects*)!

Eriskay, Western Isles

KEY

□	RS: knit WS: purl
•	RS: purl WS: knit
ꙇ	corn stitch
⟍⟍	Cable 2 Left
⟍	skp
⟋	k2tog
o	yarnover

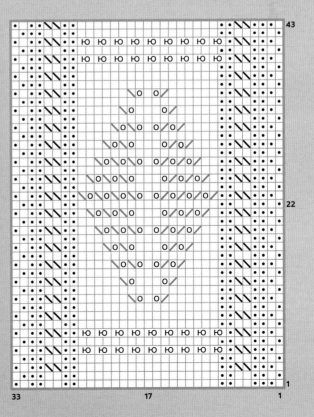

HERRINGBONES

REFLECTING THE FISHING HERITAGE

The Gansey is so linked to herring fishing, that it is not surprising some of the finest designs represent the 'silver darling', as it is affectionately known in Scotland. I imagine that as the herring girls spent their days gutting fish, it is not surprising their knitting was also full of fish bones! We saw the most ornate patterns in the north east of Scotland, including some with extra decoration. Sheila notes that the Inverness pattern displays an extra squared off diamond symbol, which gives it a different look altogether. Worked both in horizontal bands and in vertical bands, these chevrons are very effective. These shapes and patterns also relate to the classic woven fabrics of several areas around the coast, including the wonderful Harris Tweed® from the Hebrides.

SMALL HERRINGBONES

Leith, Edinburgh

KEY

☐ RS: knit   WS: purl

▪ RS: purl   WS: knit

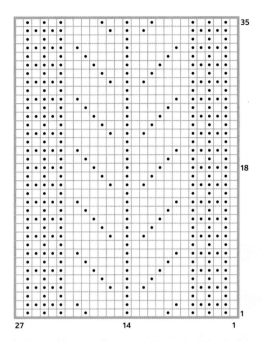

Fife

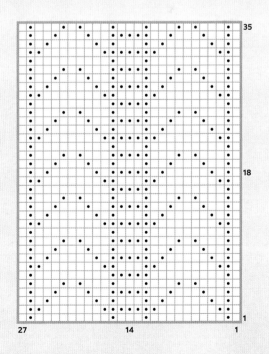

63

HERRINGBONE PATTERNS

Filey, Yorkshire

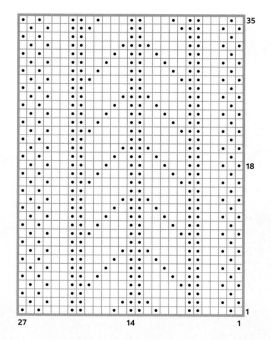

Polperro, Cornwall

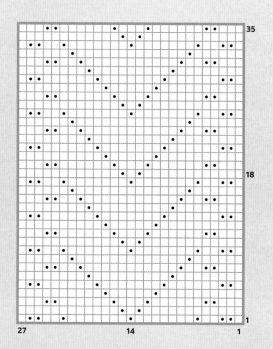

Inverness, Highlands

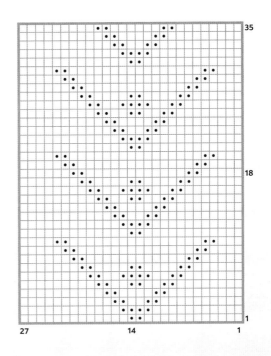

Fraserburgh, Aberdeenshire

Hopeman, Moray Firth

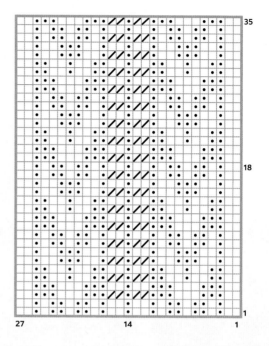

Scottish Fleet

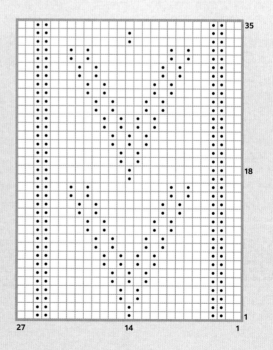

LARGE HERRINGBONES

KEY

| | RS: knit | WS: purl | | Cable 2 Right |
| | RS: purl | WS: knit | |

Scottish Fleet 1

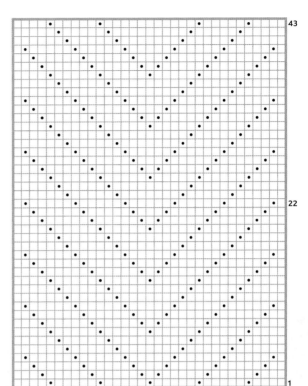

Scottish Fleet 2

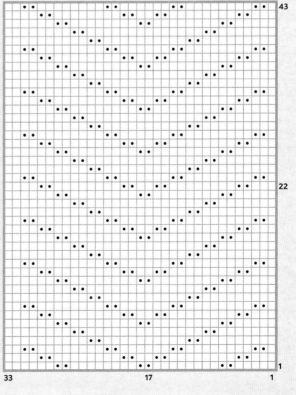

HERRINGBONE PATTERNS

ZIGZAGS

UPS AND DOWNS

Zigzags have many names. Marriage lines describe the ups and downs of married life. The Road to Duffus describes the winding track down the cliffs to the village. They are very interesting and special and form a great part of the Scottish tradition. Often separated by really complex seeding sections in great vertical bands, they are extremely effective. Some are quite simple with a single stitch, others are travelling pairs of stitches. One of my favourites is a band of moss stitches making an almost ribbon-like zigzag, which creates a great fabric.

SMALL ZIGZAGS

☐ RS: knit   WS: purl

• RS: purl   WS: knit

Scottish Fleet

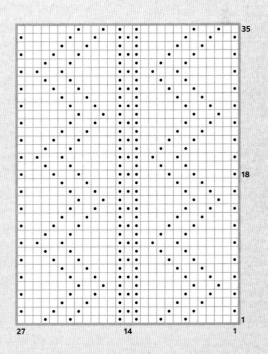

Fife

LARGE ZIGZAGS

Eriskay, Western Isles

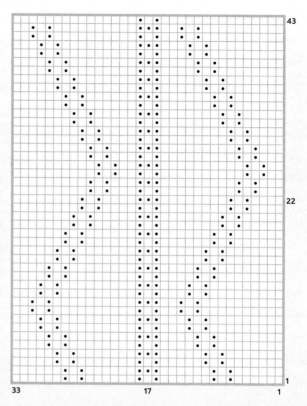

Rosemarkie, Aberdeenshire

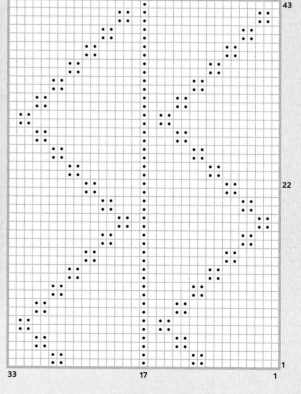

□ RS: knit WS: purl
⊡ RS: purl WS: knit

Wick, Caithness

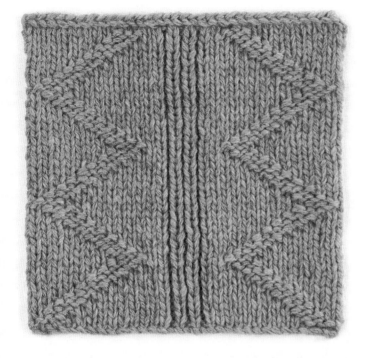

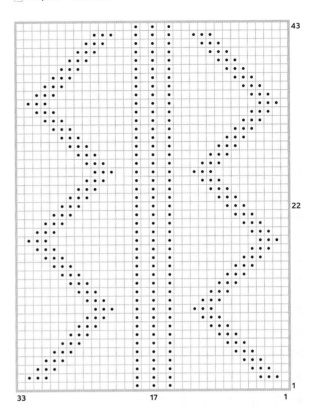

Whitehills, Aberdeenshire

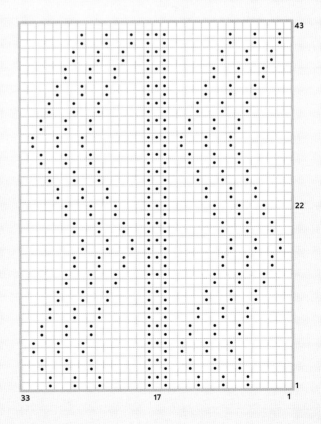

71

ZIGZAG PATTERNS

Arbroath Marriage Lines, Angus

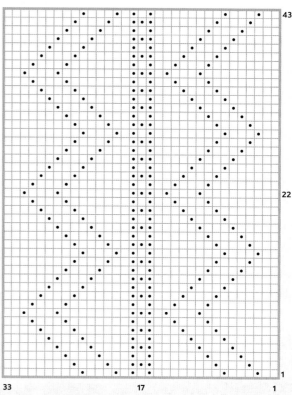

Anstruther, Fife

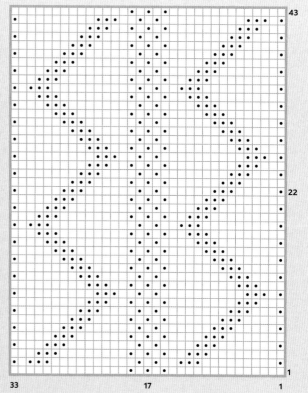

KEY

☐ RS: knit   WS: purl

• RS: purl   WS: knit

Northumberland

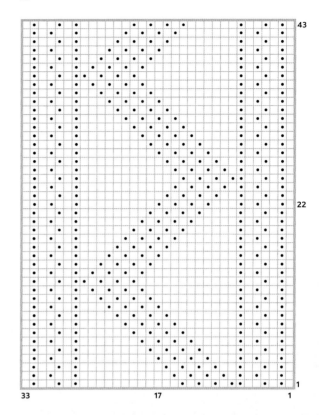

Filey, Yorkshire

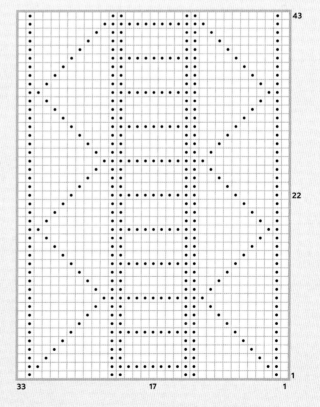

FLAGS AND ANCHORS

LIKE A RIPPLE ON THE WATER

Flags are one of our favourite patterns! In Scotland we discovered the flags used as an all-over design that almost made a fabric in itself, showing a wonderful rippling effect like the surface of the sea. Flags are also used in vertical columns, sometimes flanked with trees (see *Pattern Directory: Tree of Life*), or with cables and seed patterns. Flags were raised by the fishing fleet as the boats entered the harbours they would visit on their journey following the herring down the east coast of Scotland, starting in Shetland, and England. The flags identified the individual boats to the harbour master.

One of the greatest anchor designs is from Wick, Caithness (also see it included as a special pattern in *Pattern Directory: Heapies*). We have found some incredible anchor patterns from the north of Scotland and this one is of particular note; complex and detailed, knitted with great accuracy and knowledge. It is very difficult working only with knit and purl stitches to achieve such intricate definition of line and shows the hand of a tremendous knitter.

FLAGS

Scottish Coast

KEY

☐ RS: knit   WS: purl

• RS: purl   WS: knit

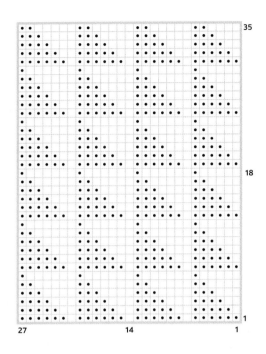

Fife

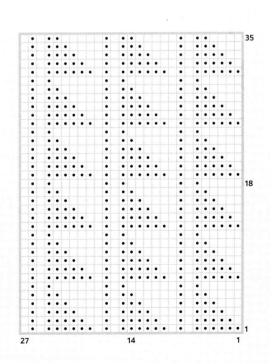

Scottish Coast

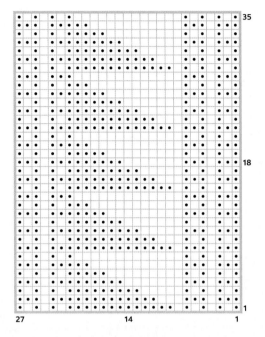

Fraserburgh, Aberdeenshire

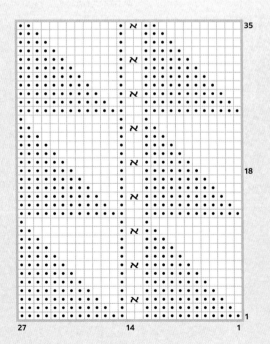

ANCHORS

KEY

□ RS: knit   WS: purl   Mock Cable

• RS: purl   WS: knit

Wick, Caithness

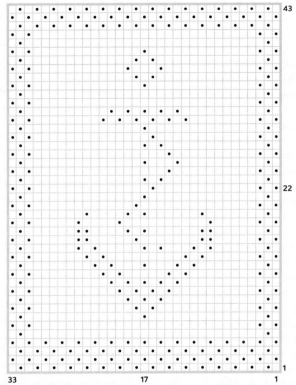

Fraserburgh, Aberdeenshire

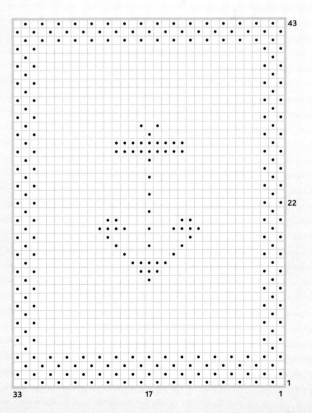

Fife

KEY

☐ RS: knit   WS: purl

• RS: purl   WS: knit

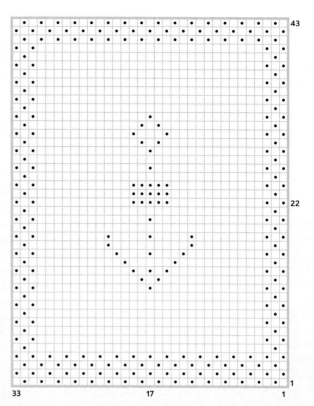

Eriskay, Western Isles

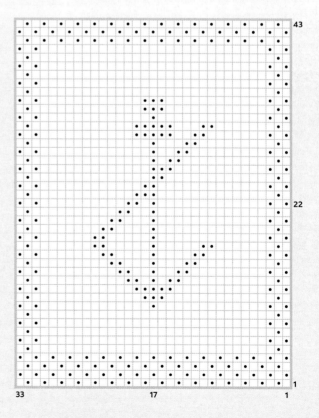

NEWBIGGIN, NORTHUMBERLAND

This is such a cracker of a design we just had to add it as one of our 'special' patterns. It falls into so many categories: triangles, flags, zigzags and marriage lines. It is one of those designs that looks one way in a certain light and in another light quite different. Flanked by regular cables and a classic moss stitch seeding section, I just love it. It reminds me of garlands and ribbons and seems both striking and celebratory.

Newbiggin, Northumberland

KEY

☐ RS: knit	WS: purl
▣ RS: purl	WS: knit
╱ ╱	Cable 6 Right

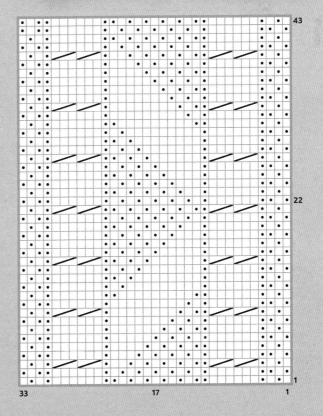

TRELLISES

CONFIDENT BANDED DESIGNS

Many Ganseys have wide spectacular horizontal patterns that are extremely geometric and look tremendous, often divided by sections of 'rig and furrow' to add to their impact. These are confident designs and we have found them in many areas along the coasts. The Scottish Fleet designs in the Fisheries Museum are all beautiful, including the large herringbone and diamond trellis. There is also a diamond and 'rig and furrow' design from Foula, Shetland, although there is little evidence of a long history of Gansey knitting there. However, as we have noted, crews and herring girls travelled all over the country resulting in mixed styles in various garments.

The Humber Ganseys have some very distinct features and one is the wonderful extended zigzag pattern.

The Cornish weave designs stand on their own. These horizontal patterns are great extensions of their seeding patterns and create an overall fabric, rather than a series of symbols.

Often described as relatively simple, they are in fact extremely clever and beautiful, and create wide horizontal bands that seem to reflect the very nature of the sea and waters being fished. The effect of the basketweave repeating is to distort the knit, creating a moving surface to the design. They have a very contemporary feel and are less figurative than other stitch patterns, creating a rhythmic and very particular Cornish style.

KEY

☐ RS: knit   WS: purl

⊡ RS: purl   WS: knit

Polperro, Cornwall 1

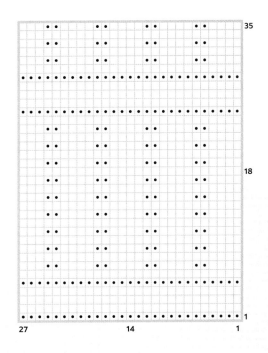

Polperro, Cornwall 2

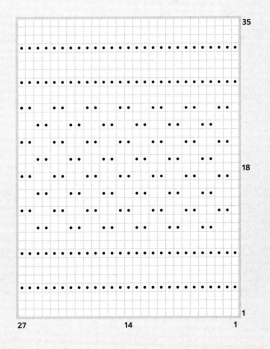

Humber River

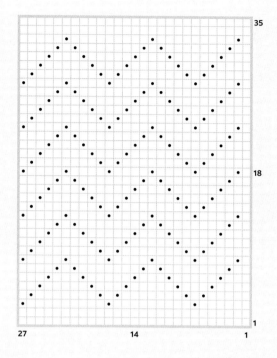

Cullercoats, Tyneside

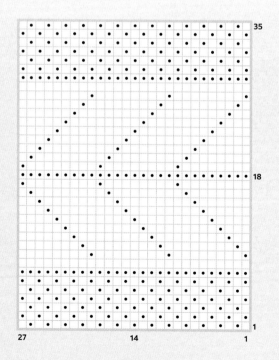

KEY

☐ RS: knit   WS: purl

⊡ RS: purl   WS: knit

Scottish Fleet 1

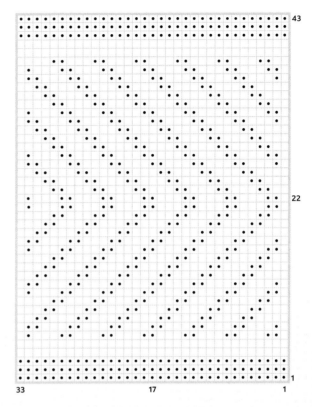

Scottish Fleet 2

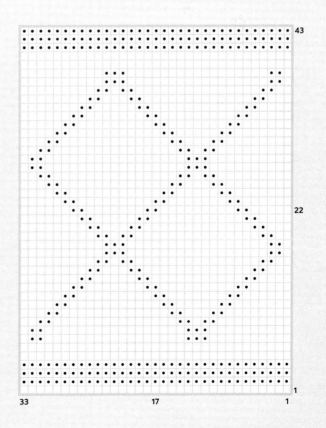

83

Scottish Fleet 3

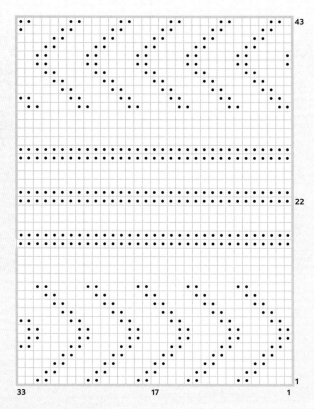

Foula, Shetland

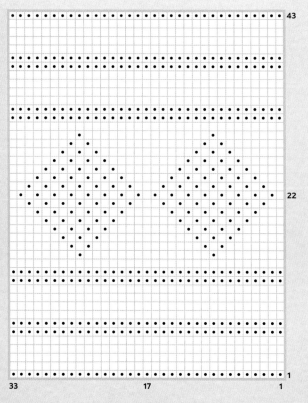

CORNISH WEAVES

KEY

☐ RS: knit   WS: purl

• RS: purl   WS: knit

Morwenstow Slate

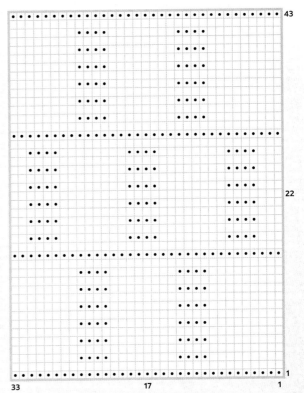

The Lizard Lattice

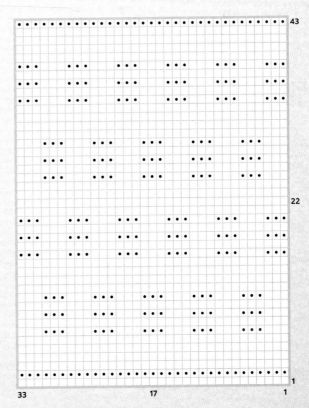

Laughing Boy

KEY

☐ RS: knit   WS: purl

• RS: purl   WS: knit

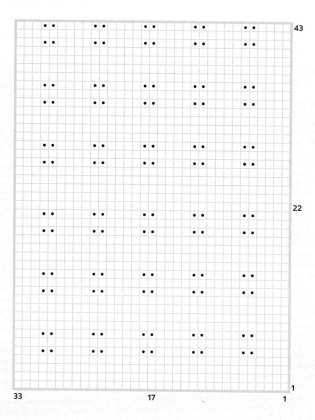

Looe, Eddystone Lighthouse

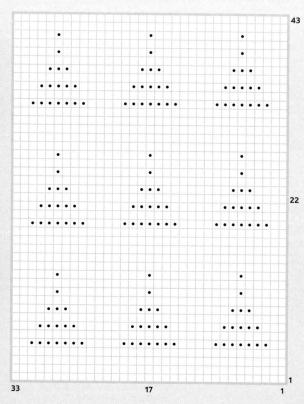

PETERHEAD CABLES AND BASKETWEAVE

This fabulous pattern we found in just one research book and it really pairs itself nicely with the Pittenweem stitch pattern. It is a unique use of a mixture of basketweave, worked in double moss stitch, with offset large cables to create a unique 'fabric' in a vertical design set on a stocking (stockinette) stitch background. The basketweaves are often overlooked as a rather old-fashioned design. Through our journey of discovery while recording garments as part of the 'Knitting the Herring' project and on the Moray Firth Partnership Gansey project we have found these apparently simple designs to be far more interesting and complex than we could have ever imagined, creating texture, ripples, waves, horizontally, vertically, and as seeding patterns. They really show the inventiveness of these amazing knitters from all around the coast!

Peterhead

KEY

☐ RS: knit   WS: purl

• RS: purl   WS: knit

Cable 10 Left

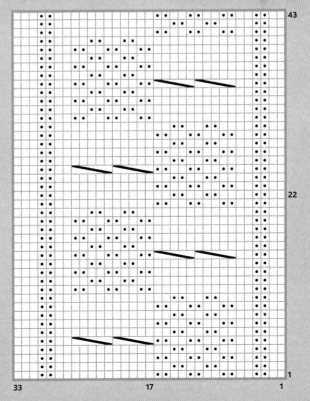

SEEDING

THE KNITTER'S SIGNATURE

The importance of these 'joining' patterns used by knitters up and down the coast cannot be underestimated and in my view shows more than anywhere else the hand of the knitter. Gansey knitting is all about the individual and their use of stitches known within each family and passed down over the generations (see *A Short History of Ganseys*).

Mrs Elsie Buchan, whose beautiful Ganseys are a part of the Moray Firth Collection, was a fabulous knitter. She used the 2-stitch mock cable in a variety of ways to create something very special and seen nowhere else. In the samples from Elsie we see the single, double and double-double mock cables in a 2-, 4- or 6-row repeat. She also sometimes used a purl stitch to separate the double-double mock cables and sometimes not. This shows her great experience and ingenuity, to create a rippled and delicate pattern that highlights the vertical patterns from the north east perfectly. Combined with diamonds, chevrons and flags they are truly unique.

Other commonly found seeding patterns in Scotland have elements of rib, moss stitch, garter stitch bars and 2-stitch cables. We will be exploring these in this section and looking at the progressions knitters used to add stitches to their patterning to adjust the size of a garment.

SEEDING CABLE PROGRESSIONS

KEY

☐ RS: knit   WS: purl   ⧄ Cable 2 Right

• RS: purl   WS: knit   И Mock Cable

Aberdeenshire Small Cables Progressions

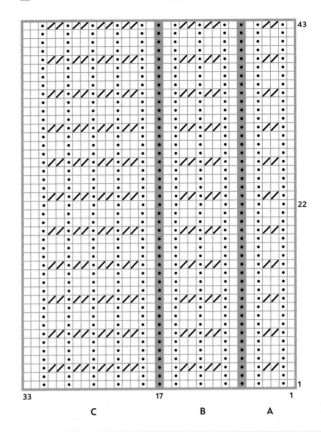

C   B   A

Aberdeenshire Mock Cables Progressions

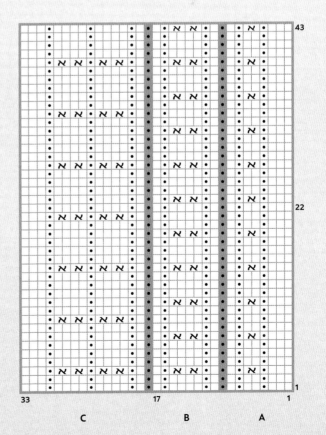

C   B   A

BASKETWEAVES AND STEPS

The small basketweaves and steps used as seeding patterns are a delight and clearly show the hand of the knitter and the way the knitter was thinking as she created her Gansey. Sheila was particularly struck when knitting the progressions at the variety of different effects you can achieve by simply having blocks of stitches in different relationships to themselves. The Cornish examples seem different again, as they often have a row in between that opens out the fabric. The ingenuity of the knitters in changing simply the number of rows or stitches to give a different effect and then matching them up with cables is incredible.

East Coasts 1

B   A

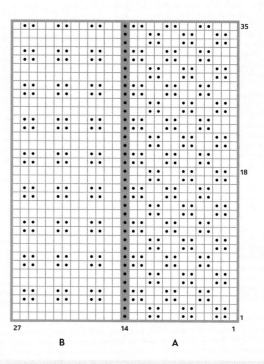

B   A

East Coasts 2

B   A

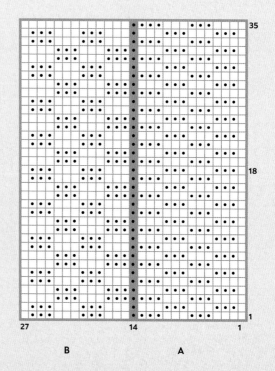

B   A

KEY

☐ RS: knit   WS: purl

⊡ RS: purl   WS: knit

East Coasts 3

B   A

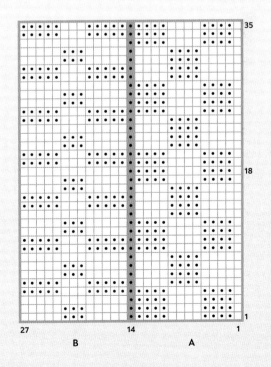

East Coasts 4

B   A

SEEDING PATTERNS

KEY

☐ RS: knit   WS: purl

▣ RS: purl   WS: knit

All Coasts 1

B   A

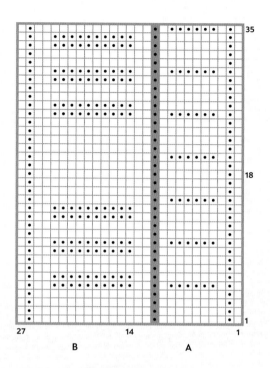

B   A

All Coasts 2

C   B   A

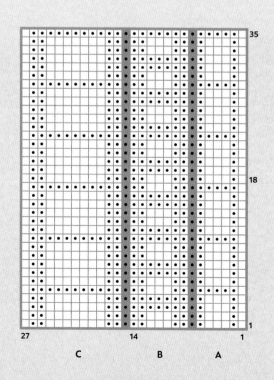

C   B   A

LARGE STEPS

The clearest steps we have seen as major patterns - not counting those in seeding sections - come from Filey in Yorkshire and Bude in Cornwall. They are both very distinctive and I so loved the Bude steps pattern that it became the basis for the *Sea Biscuit Cardigan* (see *Projects*).

Filey, Yorkshire

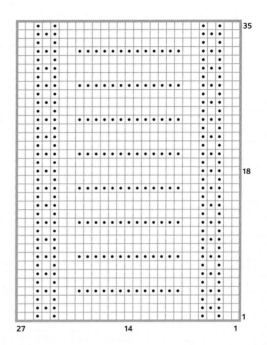

Bude, Cornwall

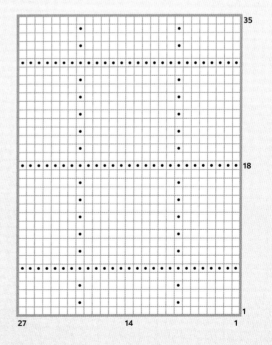

SEEDING PATTERNS

BARS

These patterns all come from the north east coast of Scotland, and may represent sand bars at the entrances to harbours. Created by the particular flow of the North Sea currents, the shifting bars of sand often signal a tricky place for sailors to navigate. From a knitter's perspective, bars provide a diagonal alternative to steps and ladders.

Buckie, Aberdeenshire

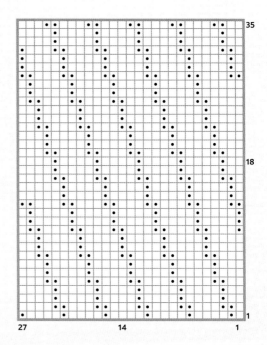

Eriskay, Western Isles

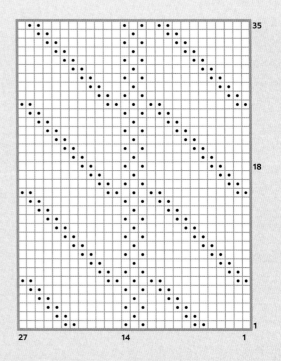

KEY

☐ RS: knit   WS: purl

• RS: purl   WS: knit

Arbroath, Angus

Fife

SEEDING PATTERNS

RIBS AND MOSS

We have collected four lots of seeding pattern progressions to show how knitters could work these 'joining' designs to add in or take away stitches easily. Some of these are quite distinctive and well known, others less so. One of the Cornish ribs shows a very rare use of a slip stitch. I also love the broken lines of those of the east coast, which again distort the knitting with a ripple effect.

East Coasts 1

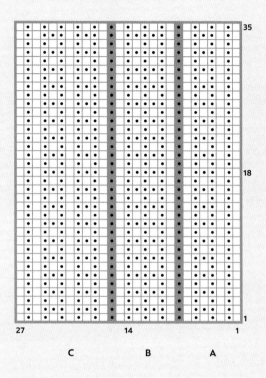

East Coasts 2

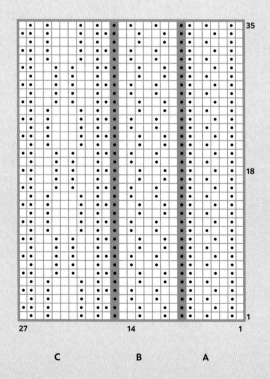

KEY

☐ RS: knit   WS: purl

• RS: purl   WS: knit

V slip stitch

Cornish Ribs

C   B   A

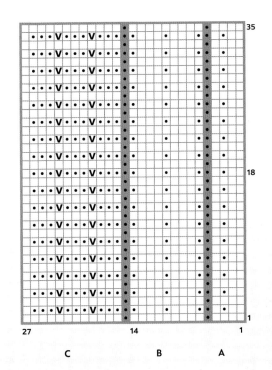

27   14   1

C   B   A

All Coasts

C   B   A

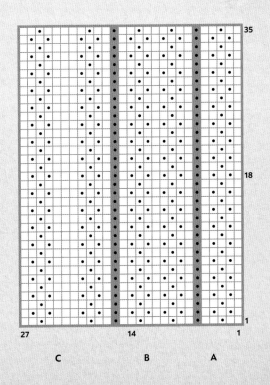

27   14   1

C   B   A

HEAPIES

SPECIAL WEE TRIANGLES

I discovered the word 'heapies', used to describe the triangular
patterns found in many Ganseys, some years ago and set out
on a quest to discover where the word came from. The word is
used in many books for many different areas, but in my search I
found that it originated in an area of northern Scotland, Buchan,
and I have dedicated a section to the story in the *History* chapter
(see *Pattern origins*).

KEY

☐ RS: knit   WS: purl

• RS: purl   WS: knit

Wick, Caithness 1

Wick, Caithness 2

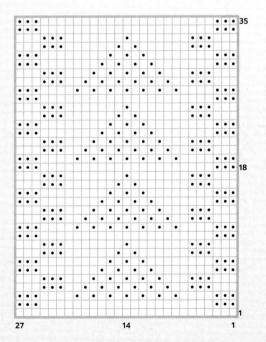

KEY

☐ RS: knit   WS: purl

⊡ RS: purl   WS: knit

Wick, Caithness 3

Peterhead, Aberdeenshire

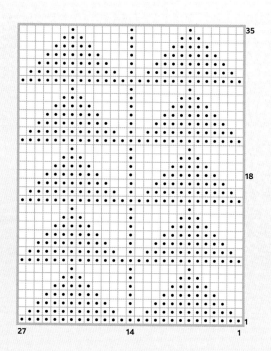

WICK ANCHOR AND HEAPIES

Wick Ganseys are some of the most complex and interesting of all. This beautiful, intricate anchor married to the 'wee heapies' pattern and broken moss seeding sections is a match made in heaven, please excuse the pun! The balance between the seeding sections and the grand design or symbol is perfect and the anchor itself is so cleverly thought out we could not resist marking this combination as 'special'. Following our research, Sheila and I are confident that many of the complex symbols, designs, and seeding stitches started their lives in the far north of Scotland. There is a depth of knowledge in the work that shines through. The knitters have worked out exactly how the purl stitch reacts when set against a knit stitch, where it disappears from view and where it can be worked to its greatest advantage.

These designs were often knitted at incredibly tight tension (gauge) of more than 60 stitches per 10cm/4in to enable the more complex designs to show clearly. These Ganseys are quite light to wear, warm, dense, and highly durable, yet not stiff.

Wick Anchor and Heapies

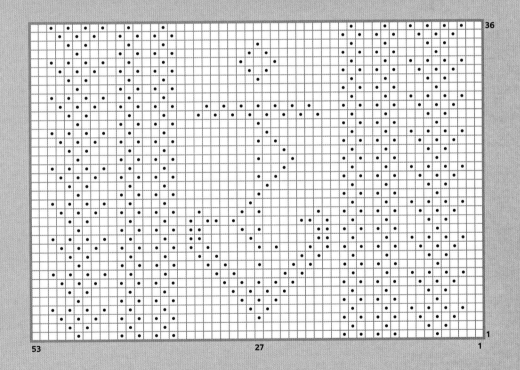

HEARTS AND STARS

A MESSAGE TO THE WEARER

Hearts appear rarely in Gansey knitting, but when they do appear, they are really quite special. There are two designs from the north and east of Scotland that are used as vertical main bands, interspersed with seeding patterns.

In other areas of the British Isles hearts are often knitted into the gusset or just above the welt of the garment, maybe as a special sign to the wearer from the person who made it with love for them. A heart is the perfect symbol to add to our beautiful Gansey cardigan design, especially if you are knitting it for someone else!

The star design stands out on its own, seen only in Eriskay and the Humber Ganseys. After much consideration we think it could reflect the long tradition of contract knitting in Scotland and particularly the islands where Aran, Fair Isle and lace designs were made for sale in Ireland, London and around the world. It would not take a lot to translate a Fair Isle/Scandanavian star design, originally worked in colour, into Gansey stitch work.

The starfish are also quite distinct and representational; these enigmatic designs are only seen in the Ganseys from Eriskay in the Western Isles. I remember collecting the lobster pot I kept attached to Pooltiel Pier on Skye when I lived in a cottage looking over the harbour, to find it full of huge starfish and my lobster hollowed out and yet weirdly intact. Small boat crab and lobster fishermen would be very familiar with the starfish. On their good advice, I never let my pot stay down more than a tide before checking it again.

HEARTS

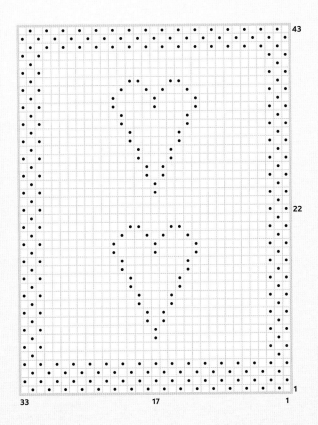

KEY

☐ RS: knit   WS: purl

● RS: purl   WS: knit

Flamborough, Yorkshire

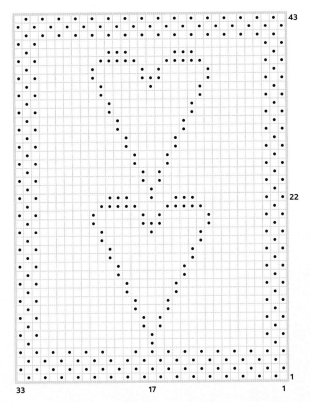

Fraserburgh, Aberdeenshire

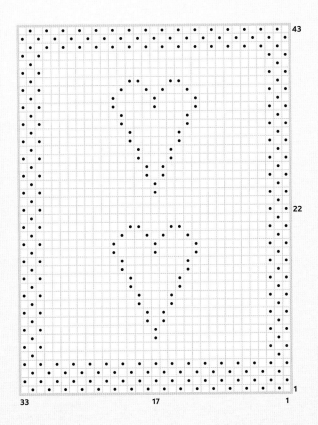

Filey, Yorkshire

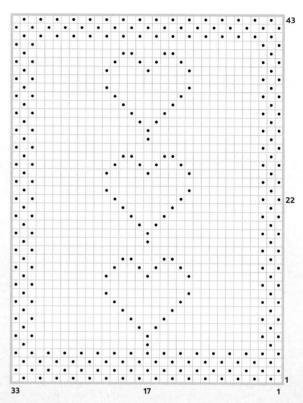

Fife

STARS

KEY

☐ RS: knit   WS: purl

• RS: purl   WS: knit

Humber Star

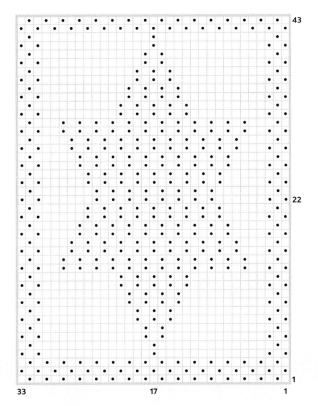

Eriskay, Western Isles

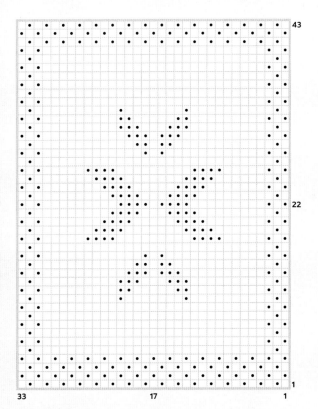

STARFISH

Eriskay, Western Isles 1

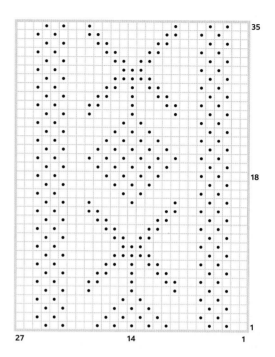

Eriskay, Western Isles 2

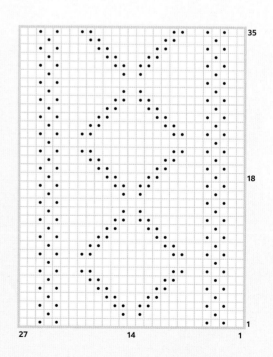

SHERINGHAM CRAB POTS

Sheila and I, at just about the same moment, spotted something not quite right in my Bible, i.e. Gladys Thompson's book on Ganseys. I remember many years ago spotting the first mistake in the Print O' the Hoof design, which I worked and reworked until I had to admit that it was wrong. I bought this book as a child and it has accompanied me throughout my life, so finding any mistake was a big deal. This new problem was a challenge and I found it fascinating. I trained as an historian, I had been taught the importance of primary source material in the understanding of an historical narrative.

Looking up at us from the page was a perfect example of how a primary source had been misinterpreted and had led to more than 50 years of misrepresentation! The primary source was the photograph of a Gansey but the chart, we realized, did not match the knitting. The fine design on the Gansey had been watered down and simplified. We were both sitting in a tent in the rain on a film set with nothing better to do than look in detail at the samples we were working on. It was another moment of incredulous gasps. I drew a new chart and when Sheila knitted it up we understood how important it was. This was not a simple triangle but a complex and very specific net design with diamonds. I started researching. The wrong chart was in every book following on from Thompson's. I looked up Sheringham and found an answer. Martin Warren, as passionate as we are, had also discovered the discrepancy. We were looking at a special crab cage used in this one small part of the country. Highly descriptive, just like the 'heapies' of Buchan; evidence that knitters created special designs to reflect day to day life. Nowhere else does this crab pot design appear. So often with history the recording of primary source material is incorrect and leads to misdirection and misunderstanding. Thanks to Martin for confirming and putting my mind at rest!

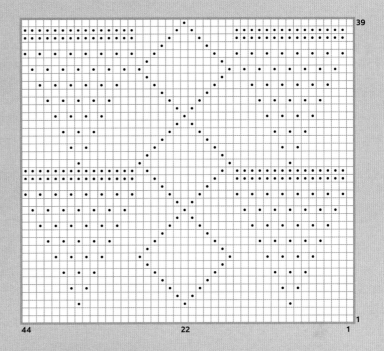

Sheringham Crab Pots

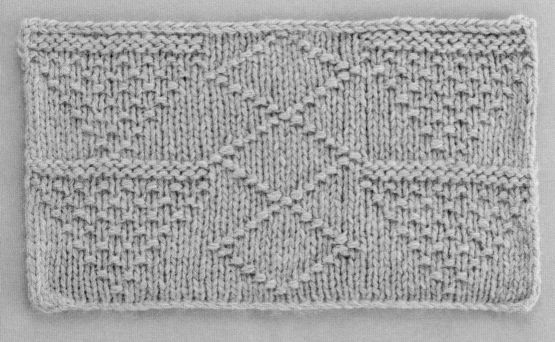

PROJECTS

Buchan

CHILD'S GANSEY

A PERFECT WEE GANSEY FOR BABIES AND TODDLERS, WITH A NECK FLAP WITH BUTTON TO
ALLOW FOR EASY WEAR, AND KNITTED IN THE TRADITIONAL WAY. THESE BEAUTIFUL PATTERNS
ARE MOSTLY FROM THE EAST NEUK OF FIFE; ZIGZAGS, HERRINGBONE AND PARALLEL LINES,
ALONG WITH A VERY SPECIAL 'SEEDING' PATTERN. I PARTICULARLY LOVE THE COLOUR OF THESE
GANSEYS AS THEY REPLICATE ONE OF OUR FAVOURITES FROM THE MORAY FIRTH COLLECTION
KNITTED BY MRS ELSIE BUCHAN, WHO WAS A FABULOUS KNITTER AND USED A WHOLE VARIETY
OF COLOURS IN HER BEAUTIFUL GANSEYS.

YARN

Quince & Co. Lark (100% wool), 10ply/
aran/worsted, 50g (123m/134yds)

3 (4) 5 hanks

Shown in Sage (size B) and
Chanterelle (size C)

TENSION (GAUGE)

24 stitches and 30 rows/rounds
measure 10 x 10cm/4 x 4in over pattern
using 4mm needles

NEEDLES & ACCESSORIES

1 set of 4mm (US 6) double-pointed
needles for body and sleeves

1 pair of 4mm (US 6) straight needles
for front and back sections worked
straight after armhole divide,
and at neck

1 button

Waste yarn or stitch holders

Stitch markers (optional)

Tapestry (darning) needle

CONSTRUCTION

The two welts are worked in rows on straight needles and then joined after the side slits to continue working in the round in the traditional way with underarm gussets. At the armholes the garment divides for a Front and Back and is worked in rows on straight needles. The shoulders are joined with an external 3-needle cast off, then the neck flap with buttonhole is worked. The sleeve stitches are picked up and worked along with the gusset stitches. The flexibility of this seeding pattern helps in creating the different sizes of the garment and is used in the welt, on the cuff and at the shoulder and neck.

MAKE YOUR OWN VERSION

If you would like to add your own signature patterns, choose from the wonderful patterns in the *Pattern Directory* of this book! The Gansey for size B is knitted with the Fife parallel lines pattern (charts 1A and 5A), while the Gansey for size C is knitted with Scottish parallel lines (charts 1B and 5B), just to show how you can change the overall look quite easily. You can also adjust the sizing by adding or taking away the 'seeding' sections, which have been placed so that this is easy to do.

KEY

- ☐ RS: knit WS: purl
- ☐ RS: purl WS: knit
- ☐ Repeat
- ☐ Start/end for size A
- ☐ Start/end for size B
- ☐ Start/end for size C
- ☐ Start/end for size B & C

SEEDING STITCH CHART
2 sts by 2 row Repeat

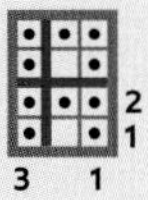

CHART 1A
11 (13, 15) sts by 12 row Repeat

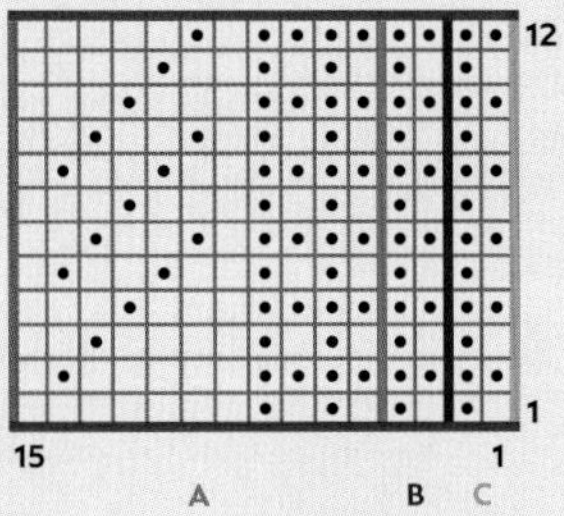

CHART 1B
11 (13, 15) sts by 12 row Repeat

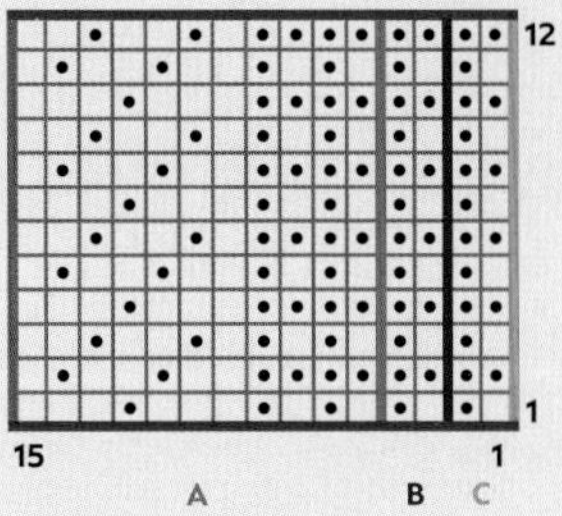

CHART 2
14 (16, 16) sts by 10 row Repeat

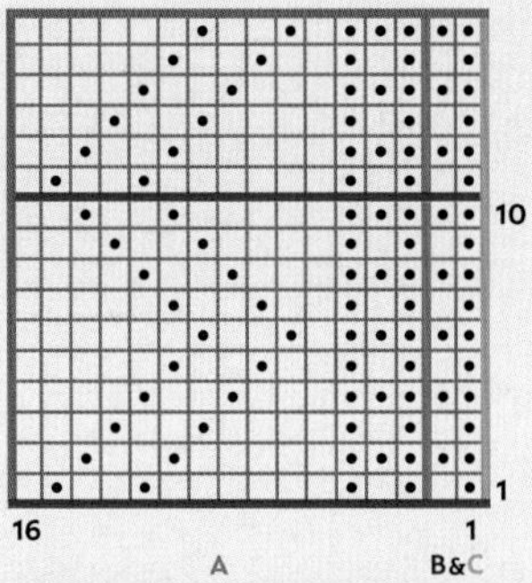

CHART 3
17 (21, 25) sts by 4 row Repeat

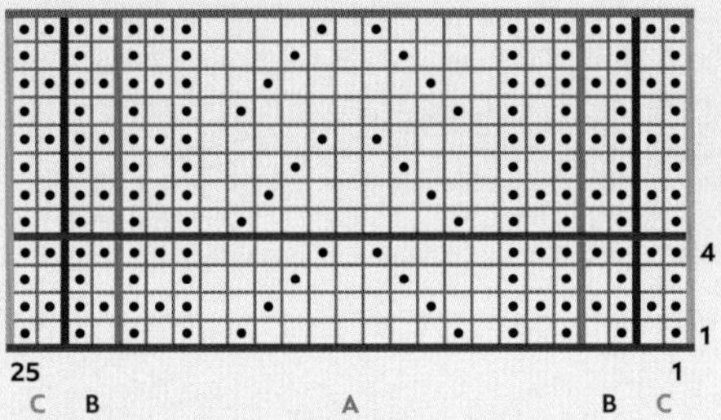

CHART 4
14 (16, 16) sts by 10 row Repeat

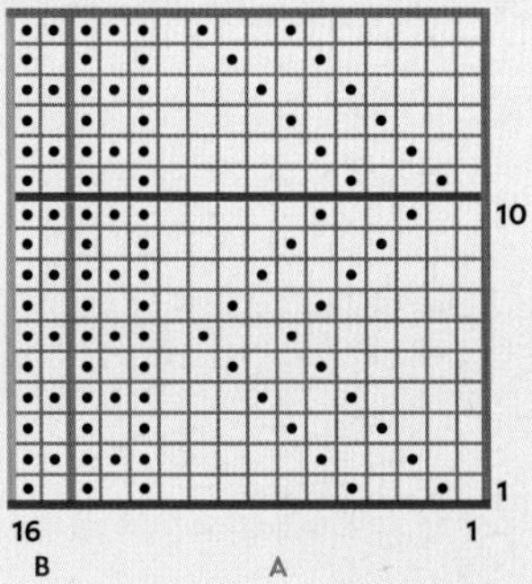

CHART 5A
10 (12, 14) sts by 12 row Repeat

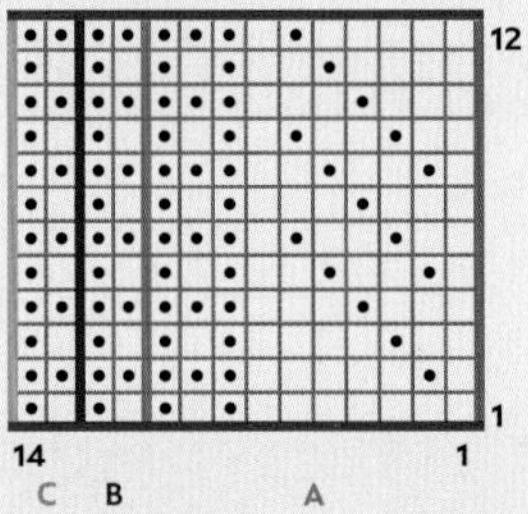

CHART 5B
10 (12, 14) sts by 12 row Repeat

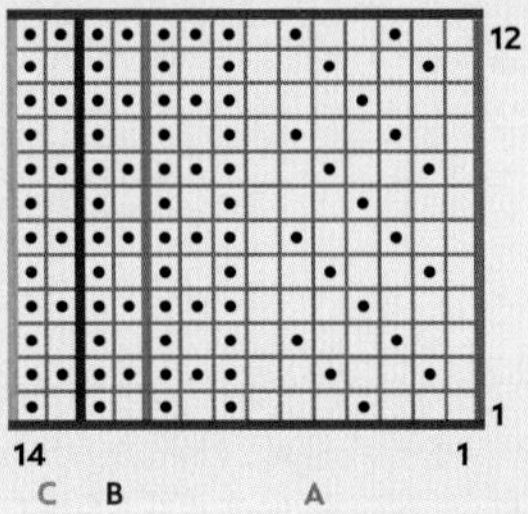

SIZE	TO FIT CHEST	BACK WIDTH	LENGTH TO SIDE SHOULDER	LENGTH TO UNDERARM	ARMHOLE DEPTH (INCLUDING GUSSET)	BACK NECK WIDTH	SLEEVE LENGTH	CUFF CIRCUMFERENCE
A: 6-12M	46cm (18in)	27.5cm (10¾in)	24cm (9½in)	12cm (4¾in)	12cm (4¾in)	15.5cm (6in)	17.5cm (6¾in)	12.5cm (5in)
B: 1-2YRS	51cm (20in)	32.5cm (12¾in)	29cm (11½in)	15.5cm (6¼in)	13.5cm (5¼in)	18cm (7in)	20.5cm (8in)	15cm (6in)
C: 3-4YRS	58.5cm (23in)	36cm (14in)	35cm (13¾in)	20cm (7¾in)	15cm (6in)	18cm (7in)	25cm (9¾in)	17.5cm (7in)

WELTS (MAKE TWO)

Using 4mm straight needles cast on 67 (79) 87 sts using a long tail cast on.

Row 1 (WS): K1, work row 1 of Seeding Stitch chart to last st, k1.

Row 2 (RS): K1, work row 2 of Seeding Stitch chart to last st, k1.

These 2 rows set pattern and edge sts.

Work another 4 (6) 8 rows in pattern as set, do not turn.

Set sts aside on waste yarn or a stitch holder while you work the second Welt.

BODY

JOIN TO WORK IN THE ROUND

Note: Transfer sts to 4mm double-pointed needles as you work the following round.

Next round: With right side of first Welt facing, pattern to last st as set, knit next st together with the first st of the second Welt (ensure this also is right side facing), pattern across second Welt to last st, knit this st together with first st of first Welt. 132 (156) 172 sts.

Arrange sts so that you have 33 (39) 43 sts on each of your four double-pointed needles. Note that when following charts for the remainder of the pattern the chart is marked to show you how many sts to work for your size.

Set-up round: *Work row 1 of chart 1A or B, work row 1 of chart 2, work row 1 of chart 3, work row 1 of chart 4, work row 1 of chart 5A or B; repeat from * once more.

This round sets chart patterns and creates a garter stitch seam st at each side.

Continue working in pattern as set until Gansey measures 12 (15.5) 20cm/4¾ (6¼) 8in from cast-on edge.

INCREASE FOR GUSSETS

Note: When working increased sts on following rounds, new gusset sts should be worked as stocking (stockinette) stitch (knit every round) with the centre seam st also worked as stocking (stockinette) stitch once the gusset increases begin. If preferred you can place a marker in each side seam st.

Gussets are worked over 10 (14) 14 rounds of pattern, creating a gusset in each side seam as follows:

Round 1 (increase): Work across Front of Gansey to 1 st before the side seam st, M1R, k1, M1L, work across Back to 1 st before the side seam stitch, M1R, k1, M1L. 4 st increased.

Round 2: Work straight in pattern to end.

Round 3: Work across Front of Gansey to 1 st before the 3 gusset sts, M1R, k3, M1L, work across Back to 1 stitch before the 3 gusset sts, M1R, k3, M1L. 4 sts increased.

Round 4: Work straight in pattern to end.

Continue increasing on alternate rounds as set until you have 11 (15) 15 gusset stitches. 152 (184) 200 total stitches.

DIVIDE FOR FRONT AND BACK

Place 11 (15) 15 gusset sts at each side seam on waste yarn to work later when working the Sleeves.

Turn and work on last 65 (77) 85 sts for Back.

BACK

Using 4mm straight needles, continue straight until Back measures 22 (26) 32cm/8¾ (10¼) 12½in from cast-on edge, ending after a wrong side row.

Work 6 (8) 10 rows in Seeding Stitch pattern as before, ending after a wrong side row.

Leave sts on a spare needle. **

We've used a precious mother-of-pearl button selected from the buttonbox just like traditional Gansey knitters would have done

Ganseys are designed to allow lots of movement

**Choose your
own patterns
to use from the
Pattern Directory**

FRONT

Rejoin yarn with right side facing to remaining 65 (77) 85 sts and work as for Back to **.

SHOULDERS AND NECK

JOIN SHOULDERS

With the wrong side of Front and Back facing each other, and with the Front facing you, join first 14 (17) 21 sts of Left Shoulder using the 3-needle cast (bind) off method (see *General Techniques*), break yarn and fasten off.

With the wrong side of the Front and Back facing each other, and with the Back facing you, join first 5 (8) 10 sts of Right Shoulder using the 3-needle cast (bind) off method, and pattern until you have 9 (9) 11 Back sts on right needle.

Continue on these sts only for Buttonhole Flap (leaving remaining Back and Front sts on waste yarn for now).

BUTTONHOLE FLAP

Beginning with a wrong side row, work 2 rows straight in Seeding Stitch pattern.

Next row (WS): Pattern 3 (3) 4, cast (bind) off 3 sts, pattern to end, turn.

Next row (RS): Pattern to cast-off (bound-off) sts, cast on 3 stitches, pattern until you have 3 (3) 4 sts on right needle, turn.

Work another 2 rows straight in Seeding Stitch pattern on these 9 (9) 11 sts .

Next row (WS): Cast (bind) off 9 (9) 11 sts knitwise.

BACK NECK

With right side facing, rejoin yarn to 37 (43) 43 sts remaining for Back neck.

Work another 4 (4) 6 rows straight in pattern.

Cast (bind) off knitwise.

FRONT NECK

With wrong side facing, rejoin yarn to Front neck sts and cast (bind) off first 9 (9) 11 sts, pattern to end. 37 (43) 43 sts.

Work another 3 (3) 5 rows straight in pattern.

Cast (bind) off knitwise.

SLEEVES

Note: *When working the Seeding Stitch chart note that you will be working in rounds, not rows as you were for Welt and shoulders.*

With right side facing and using 4mm double-pointed needles, and beginning at centre gusset st, place marker for beginning of round, knit across first 6 (8) 8 sts for gusset, pick up and knit 34 (40) 54 sts around armhole, knit across remaining 5 (7) 7 gusset sts. 45 (55) 69 sts.

Next round (decrease): Knit to last 2 sts of gusset, k2tog, work Seeding Stitch chart to beginning of gusset, skp, knit to end of round. 2 sts decreased.

Next round: Knit to end of gusset, work Seeding Stitch chart to beginning of gusset, knit to end of round.

Repeat last 2 rounds until 35 (41) 55 sts remain.

Work 8 (14) 16 rounds straight in stocking (stockinette) stitch (knit every round).

SHAPE SLEEVES

Next round (decrease): K1, k2tog, knit to last 3 sts, skp. 2 sts decreased.

Decrease every 6th (6th) 4th round as set until 31 (37) 43 sts remain.

Continue straight in stocking (stockinette) stitch until Sleeve measures 16 (18.5) 22cm/6¼ (7¼) 8¾in from picked-up edge or 4 (6) 8 rounds less than desired final Sleeve length, working k2tog at end of final round to decrease away seam st. 30 (36) 42 sts.

Work in Seeding Stitch pattern for 4 (6) 8 rounds.

Cast (bind) off loosely and evenly.

FINISHING

Sew in any loose ends and sew on button below the shoulder flap buttonhole.

Lightly steam with iron held above the knitting and not on the fabric (see *General Techniques: Steam Setting*).

Hudson

SLEEVELESS SLIP OVER

I WANTED TO CREATE A SPECIAL TRADITIONAL GANSEY BUT WITH A FULLY MODERN FEEL FOR ALL THE MEN IN MY LIFE WHO NOW LIVE AND WORK IN URBAN ENVIRONMENTS, WHICH AT TIMES CAN FEEL AS DANGEROUS AS BEING OUT AT SEA. HUDSON CROSSES OVER INTO THIS WORLD AND CAN BE WORN AT ANY TIME, ANYWHERE, TO GIVE A FEELING OF HOME AND SAFETY, WITH THE HANDS OF THE KNITTER LEAVING THEIR MARK. IT IS LIKE A PIECE OF MEDIEVAL ARMOUR SHAPED TO THE BODY, WITH THE INCREDIBLE FLAG DESIGN TO THE FORE. THE GARMENT ALSO FEATURES OUR MOCK CABLES FROM MRS ELSIE BUCHAN AND THE LEGENDARY BETTY MARTIN LADDER STITCH PATTERN.

YARN

Frangipani 5ply Worsted Spun Guernsey Yarn (100% wool), 5ply sport, 500g (1097m/1200yds)

1 (1) 1 (1) cone

Amounts per size:
375g (400g) 435g (475g)

Shown in Cinder (size Small)

TENSION (GAUGE)

32 stitches and 42 rows/rounds measure 10 x 10cm/4 x 4in over pattern using 2.25mm needles

NEEDLES & ACCESSORIES

1 set of 2.25mm (US 1) double-pointed needles 35cm/14in long, or circular needle at least 80cm/32in long

1 pair of 2.25mm (US 1) straight needles

Waste yarn or stitch holders

Stitch markers

Tapestry (darning) needle

CONSTRUCTION

The two welts for Hudson are worked in rows on straight needles and then joined after the side slits to continue working in the round in the traditional way, up to the beginning of the armhole shaping. At the armholes the garment divides for a Front and Back and is again worked in rows on straight needles.

PATTERN NOTES

MOSS STITCH (IN THE ROUND)

Round 1: [K1, p1] to end.

Round 2: [P1, k1] to end.

These two rounds are repeated to form moss stitch.

MOSS STITCH (IN ROWS)

Row 1 (RS): [K1, p1] to end.

Row 2: As Row 1.

These two rows are repeated to form moss stitch.

ARMHOLE SHAPING

To achieve the neatest edge, work the decrease one stitch in from the armhole edge. Work a skp decrease for left-leaning edges and a k2tog decrease for right-leaning edges. Place decreases as indicated by shaped edges on charts.

SLOPING CAST (BIND) OFF FOR NECK SHAPING

Work to the last stitch on the row, do not work the stitch but slip it and turn. Slip the next stitch unworked and pass the first slipped stitch over it, knit (right side rows) or purl (wrong side rows) the next stitch and pass the last stitch over it. Cast (bind) off any further stitches as shown on chart for that row to complete shaping.

WELTS (MAKE 2)

Using 2.25mm needles, cast on 159 (173) 189 (219) sts.

Work from Welt charts for your size as follows:

Row 1 (RS): Pattern 1 (8) 1 (1) st(s) as shown on chart for your size, work 15-st pattern repeat 5 (5) 6 (7) times, work centre 7 sts of chart, work 15-st pattern repeat 5 (5) 6 (7) times, pattern 1 (8) 1 (1) st(s) as shown on chart.

Row 1 sets placement of all patterns.

Continue as set until you have worked all 12 rows of Welt chart.

SIZES M, L AND XL ONLY

Work Welt chart once more.

ALL SIZES

You have worked 12 (24) 24 (24) rows in total for Welt.

Set sts aside on waste yarn or a spare needle while you work the second Welt.

The Welt section sets the formation for the start of the Flag design in the main section of the Body.

LOWER BODY

When Welts are complete, return both sets of sts to double-pointed or circular needles and join to start working in the round.

Place markers at the beginning of the round for first side seam st, at second side seam st and to mark the centre st of each Front and Back. This will help you keep track of pattern placement as you work.

Round 1: Pattern 1 (8) 1 (1) st(s) as shown on Lower Body chart for your size, work 15-st pattern repeat 5 (5) 6 (7) times, work centre 7 sts of Front, work 15-st pattern repeat 5 (5) 6 (7) times, pattern 0 (7) 0 (0) sts, k2tog, pattern 0 (7) 0 (0) sts, work 15-st pattern repeat 5 (5) 6 (7) times, work centre 7 sts of Back, work 15-st pattern repeat 5 (5) 6 (7) times, pattern 0 (7) 0 (0) sts, k2tog (knitting together the last st of round 1 and first st of round 2). 316 (344) 376 (436) sts total; 158 (172) 188 (218) sts per Front and Back.

SIZE	TO FIT CHEST	ACTUAL CHEST CIRCUMFERENCE	LENGTH TO SIDE SHOULDER	LENGTH TO UNDERARM	ARMHOLE DEPTH	BACK NECK WIDTH
S	91-97cm (36-38in)	99cm (39in)	61cm (24in)	38cm (15in)	24cm (9½in)	15cm (6in)
M	99-104cm (39-41in)	108cm (42½in)	65cm (25½in)	41cm (16in)	24cm (9½in)	15cm (6in)
L	107-117cm (42-46in)	118cm (46½in)	68cm (26¾in)	41cm (16in)	27cm (10½in)	21cm (8¼in)
XL	119-132cm (47-52in)	137cm (54in)	68cm (26¾in)	41cm (16in)	27cm (10½in)	21cm (8¼in)

Round 2: Pattern 0 (7) 0 (0) sts, work 15-st pattern repeat 5 (5) 6 (7) times, work centre 7 sts of Front, work 15-st pattern repeat 5 (5) 6 (7) times, pattern 1 (15) 1 (1) st(s), work 15-st pattern repeat 5 (5) 6 (7) times, work centre 7 sts of Back, work 15-st pattern repeat 5 (5) 6 (7) times, pattern 0 (7) 0 (0) sts.

Round 3: Pattern 1 (8) 1 (1) sts, work 15-st pattern repeat 5 (5) 6 (7) times, work centre 7 sts of Front, work 15-st pattern repeat 5 (5) 6 (7) times, pattern 1 (15) 1 (1) st(s), work 15-st pattern repeat 5 (5) 6 (7) times, work centre 7 sts of Back, work 15-st pattern repeat 5 (5) 6 (7) times, pattern 0 (7) 0 (0) sts.

Round 3 sets placement of all patterns.

Continue as set until you have worked the 12-round repeat 6 times in total (72 rounds).

Work rounds 73 to 76 once, which acts as a seeding pattern before the next section.

UPPER BODY

Round 1: Pattern 1 (8) 1 (1) st(s) as shown on Upper Body charts for your size, work 15-st pattern repeat 5 (5) 6 (7) times, work centre 7 sts of Front, work 15-st pattern repeat 5 (5) 6 (7) times, pattern 1 (15) 1 (1) st(s), work 15-st pattern repeat 5 (5) 6 (7) times, work centre 7 sts of Back, work 15-st pattern repeat 5 (5) 6 (7) times, pattern 0 (7) 0 (0) sts.

Round 1 sets placement of all patterns.

Continue as set until you have worked the 12-round repeat 6 times in total (72 rounds).

SEPARATE FOR FRONT AND BACK

You will now work back and forth in rows for Front and Back on straight needles.

Place last 158 (172) 188 (218) sts on a spare needle or waste yarn for Back and continue on next 158 (172) 188 (218) sts only for Front.

FRONT

Work in rows throughout, following the Armhole and Neck Shapings charts for your size.

ARMHOLE SHAPING

Cast (bind) off at beginning of first 6 rows as shown on charts.

Work decreases for armholes (see Pattern Notes) as shown on charts for your size.

For sizes S and L only, ensure that you have a border of 2 stitches in stocking (stockinette) stitch at each armhole edge, ignoring any purl sts shown on chart for partial Scottish Flag patterns.

When all armhole decreases are complete you should have 101 (117) 133 (161) sts on your needles.

Continue straight, following charts until you have completed row 200 (200) 201 (201).

NECK SHAPING

Next row: Pattern to centre 7 (7) 31 (31) sts, cast (bind) off next 7 (7) 31 (31) sts, pattern to end. 47 (55) 50 (65) sts remain for each shoulder.

Shape each side of neck separately as shown on charts. 21 (21) 18 (18) sts are decreased each side.

When shaping is complete you should have 26 (34) 33 (47) sts per shoulder.

Continue straight in pattern as set until you have completed row 248 (248) 260 (260) of charts.

Leave sts on a spare needle or stitch holder.

BACK

Work as for Front without neck shaping until you have completed row 248 (248) 260 (260) of charts. 101 (117) 133 (161) sts remain for Back.

Leave sts on needle ready for the 3-needle cast (bind) off.

SHOULDER SEAMS

Using the 3-needle cast (bind) off (see *General Techniques*), join the 26 (34) 33 (47) sts of the Front and Back right shoulders. Break yarn.

Leave 49 (49) 67 (67) sts for Back neck edge live on a spare needle or waste yarn.

Using the 3-needle cast (bind) off. join the 26 (34) 33 (47) sts of the Front and Back left shoulders. Break yarn.

NECK EDGING

With 2.25mm double-pointed or circular needles, and right side facing, and beginning at Back neck, knit across 49 (49) 67 (67) sts for Back neck edge, and pick up and knit 91 (91) 95 (95) sts around Front neck. 140 (140) 162 (162) sts for neck edging.

Work moss stitch in the round (see Pattern Notes) for 4 rounds.

Cast (bind) off loosely and evenly in moss stitch.

ARMHOLES

With 2.25mm double-pointed or circular needles, pick up and knit 164 (164) 184 (184) sts around armhole.

Work moss stitch in the round for 4 rounds. Cast (bind) off loosely and evenly in moss stitch.

FINISHING

Sew in any loose ends.

Lightly steam with iron held above the knitting and not on the fabric (see *General Techniques: Steam Setting*).

KEY

☐ RS: knit	☐ WS: purl
☐ RS: purl	☐ WS: knit
☐ Work sts 5 (5) 6 (7) times	
◩ k2tog	
Ⓝ Mock Cable	
■ First st is last st of row 1	
▨ Row 1 joins Welts in the round	
▨ No stitch	

LOWER BODY CHART - SIZE S, L AND XL ONLY

Knit this section 5 times in total ending with row 72

LOWER BODY CHART - SIZE M ONLY

Knit this section 5 times in total ending on row 72

WELT CHART - SIZES S, L AND XL ONLY

WELT CHART - SIZE M ONLY

UPPER BODY CHART - SIZES S, L AND XL ONLY

UPPER BODY CHART - SIZE M ONLY

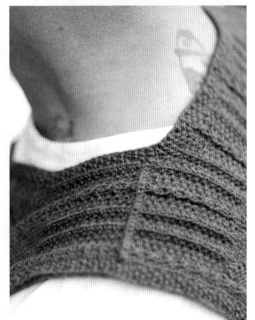

Shoulder with seaming stitch patterns and 3-needle cast (bind) off

Seeding stitch welt

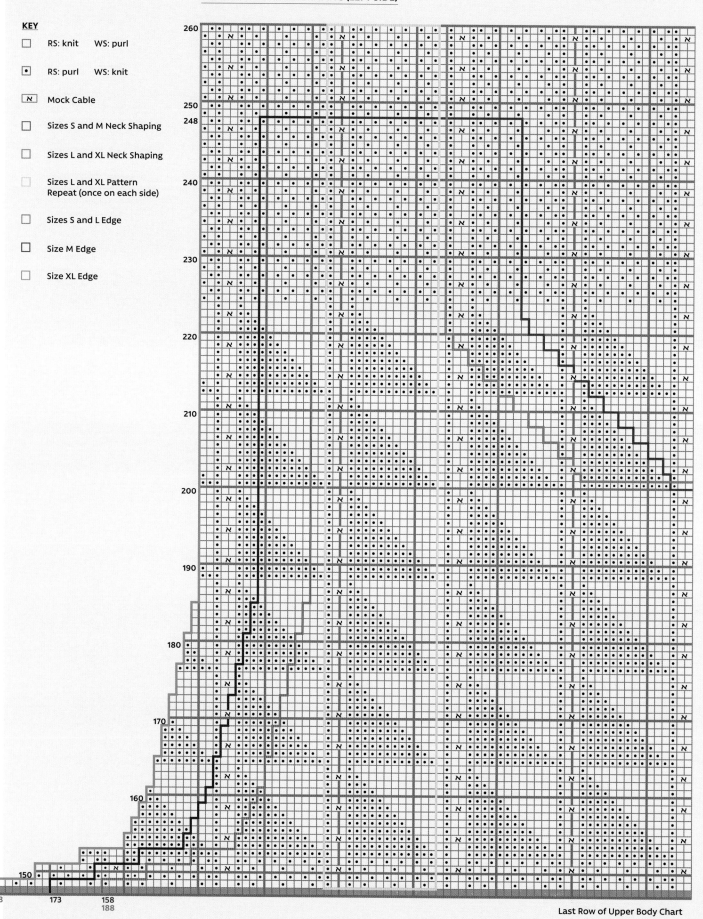

KEY

☐ RS: knit   WS: purl

⊡ RS: purl   WS: knit

N Mock Cable

☐ Sizes S and M Neck Shaping

☐ Sizes L and XL Neck Shaping

☐ Sizes L and XL Pattern
Repeat (once on each side)

☐ Sizes S and L Edge

☐ Size M Edge

☐ Size XL Edge

Last Row of Upper Body Chart

ARMHOLE AND NECK SHAPING (RIGHT SIDE)

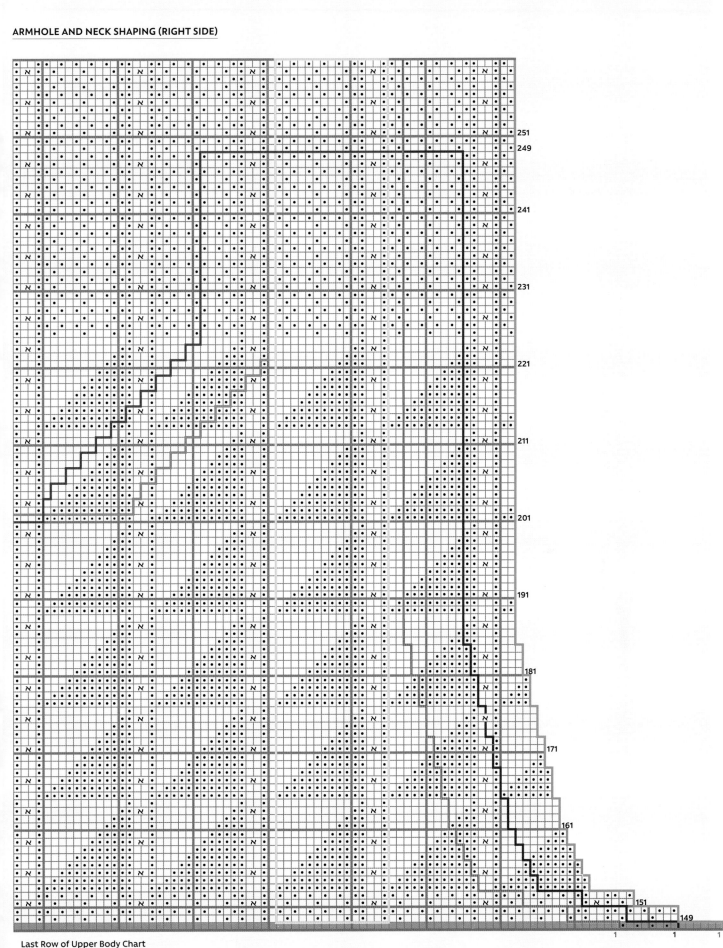

Last Row of Upper Body Chart

251
249
241
231
221
211
201
191
181
171
161
151
149

1   1   1   1

Caledonia

FINGERLESS GLOVES

CALEDONIA IS A PERFECT WEE STORM OF A DESIGN. KNITTED IN THE ROUND WITH A BEAUTIFUL THUMB GUSSET (SEE **GANSEY TECHNIQUES: GUSSETS**), SEVERAL DEVICES AND PATTERNS ARE USED TO MAKE THESE GLORIOUS. THE RIGGING PATTERN ON THE PALM OF THE HAND TIGHTENS THIS SECTION TO GIVE EXTRA WARMTH AND SHAPING, AND GIVES EXTRA GRIP TO THE GLOVES. THE MAIN MOTIF IS THE TREE OF LIFE, FOUND IN THE EAST NEUK OF FIFE, WITH A FRINGE OF DIAMONDS AND A MOSS STITCH EDGING TO THE CUFF AND TOP EDGE.

YARN

Di Gilpin Lalland Aran (100% wool), 10ply/Aran/worsted, 100g (150m/164yds)

1 (1) ball

Shown in Firebird and in Kingfisher (both size S/M)

TENSION (GAUGE)

20 stitches and 26 rows/rounds measure 10 x 10cm/4 x 4in over pattern using 4.5mm needles (size S/M)

18 stitches and 23 rows/rounds measure 10 x 10cm/4 x 4in over pattern using 5mm needles (size L/XL)

NEEDLES & ACCESSORIES

1 set of 4.5mm (US 7) double-pointed needles 20cm/8in long or short circular needle (size S/M)

1 set of 5mm (US 8) double-pointed needles 20cm/8in long or short circular needle (size L/XL)

Cable needle

Stitch marker

Tapestry (darning) needle

Tree of Life pattern

CONSTRUCTION

This project is worked from charts, and also has a moss stitch edging top and bottom, described below. The thumb gusset is worked at the same time as the hand and then cast (bound) off on round 38 of the chart.

PATTERN NOTES

WORKING FROM THE CHARTS

When working from charts the sections between red lines should be repeated the given number of times before continuing with the rest of the stitches for that row of the chart.

MOSS STITCH (IN THE ROUND)

Round 1: [K1, p1] to end.

Round 2: [P1, k1] to end.

Round 3: As round 1.

These three rounds form moss stitch.

FINGERLESS GLOVES (MAKE 1 RIGHT GLOVE AND 1 LEFT GLOVE)

Using 4.5mm (5mm) needles, cast on 40 sts, using thumb or long tail cast on.

Now join to start working in the round and place a marker at the beginning of the round.

CUFF

Work rounds 1 to 2 of moss stitch (see Pattern Notes).

Round 3 (decrease): [K1, p1] to last 2 sts, k2tog. 39 sts.

BEGIN WORKING CHART

Make sure to use the correct chart for the hand you are working on.

Work rounds 1 to 37 of Right Hand or Left Hand chart, noting that you will be working increases for the thumb gusset on rounds 21, 25 and 29.

When all thumb gusset increases have been worked you should have 47 sts on your needles.

RIGHT GLOVE ONLY

Round 38: Pattern 37 sts as set on chart, cast (bind) off next 10 sts for thumb. 37 sts for right glove.

LEFT GLOVE ONLY

Round 38: Cast (bind) off 10 sts for thumb, pattern to end of round as set on chart. 37 sts for left glove.

BOTH GLOVES

Round 39: Pattern to end, pulling yarn tight across gap created by cast-off (bound-off) sts.

Continue working in the round until you have completed round 47 of chart.

Round 48: Knit to end, increasing 1 st at end of round. 38 sts.

TOP EDGE

Work rounds 1 to 3 of moss stitch.

Cast (bind) off, not too tightly.

TO MAKE UP

Sew in any loose threads.

Lightly steam with iron held above the knitting and not on the fabric (see *General Techniques: Steam Setting*).

SIZE	NEEDLE SIZE	TO FIT HAND CIRCUMFERENCE	ACTUAL CIRCUMFERENCE	FINISHED LENGTH
S/M	4.5mm (US 7)	18-20cm (7-8in)	20cm (8in)	21cm (8¼in)
L/XL	5mm (US 8)	20-22cm (8-8½in)	22cm (8½in)	23cm (9in)

Thumb gusset

GLOVE LEFT AND RIGHT CHARTS

Left Hand

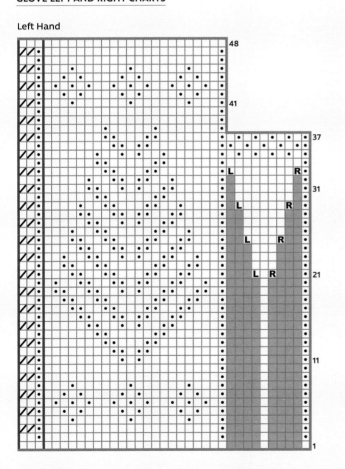

Right Hand

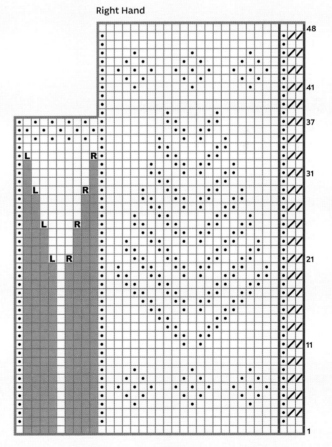

KEY

☐ RS: knit WS: purl	Ⓛ M1L	▨ Cable 2 Right
⊡ RS: purl WS: knit	Ⓡ M1R	▨ No stitch

| Repeat 5 times

Nancy
GANSEY COWL

THE NANCY NAMED HERE IS FROM ONE OF MY FAVOURITE LOVE POEMS BY ROBERT BURNS. "AE FOND KISS AND THEN WE SEVER", WHICH BURNS WROTE AND SENT TO AGNES CRAIG, WHO WAS ALSO KNOWN AS NANCY, HIS UNREQUITED LOVE. I MADE THE SNOOD WITH HER IN MIND! THE HEART IS SEEN AS A VERTICAL PATTERN IN SCOTLAND BUT ALSO SEEN KNITTED INTO THE GUSSET OR NEXT TO THE WELT ON GANSEYS IN OTHER AREAS. IT OCCURS TO ME THAT THIS MAY BE THE ORIGIN OF THE PHRASE "TO WEAR YOUR HEART ON YOUR SLEEVE".

YARN

Rowan Pure Cashmere (100% cashmere), 8ply/DK light worsted, 50g (137m/150yds)

2 hanks

Shown in Lipstick

Note: A classic DK weight yarn would work as a substitute for the cashmere. We have used a slightly smaller needle than recommended to give an extra 'pop' to the Gansey stitches.

TENSION (GAUGE)

24 stitches and 32 rounds measure 10 x 10cm/4 x 4in over pattern using 3.25mm needles

NEEDLES & ACCESSORIES

1 set 3.25mm (US 3) double-pointed needles, 20cm/8in long, or 3.25mm (US 3) circular needle, 40cm/16in long

3 stitch markers

Tapestry (darning) needle

PATTERN FEATURES

This Gansey cowl developed from the beautiful patterns of the fisherfolk of Wick in Northern Scotland. They are created with a series of chevron patterns and have a truly rhythmic quality that is also seen in some of the designs from Sheringham and even the musician's pattern from Cornwall (see *Pattern Directory: Herringbones, Polperro, Cornwall*). I started working the chevrons in different directions and added the beautiful heart design from Filey, where I spent the first few years of my life.

SIZE	One size
CIRCUMFERENCE	52.5cm (20¾in)
LENGTH	35cm (13¾in)

COWL

Using 3.25mm needles, cast on 126 sts using a long tail cast on.

Join to start working in the round and place marker for beginning of round.

Foundation round: Purl to end.

You will now work from the two charts as follows:

Round 1: *Work sts 1-10 of row 1 of chart 1 twice, work sts 21-42 of row 1 of chart 2 once, place marker; repeat from * twice more with final marker being the beginning of round marker.

Rounds 2-111: *Work sts 1-10 of next row of chart 2 twice, work sts 21-42 of next row of chart 1 once, slip marker; repeat from * twice more.

Round 112 (not shown on charts): Purl.

Cast (bind) off knitwise.

TO MAKE UP

Sew in any loose ends.

If needed, lightly steam with iron held above the knitting and not on the fabric (see *General Techniques: Steam Setting*). Do not block as this will lose the lovely stitch definition.

KEY

☐ RS: knit   WS: purl
⊡ RS: purl   WS: knit

CHART 2

CHART 1

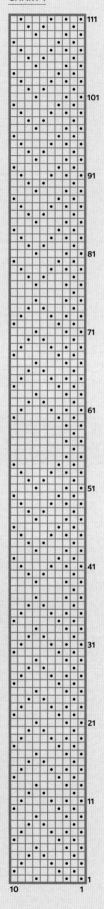

My favourite
heart pattern
from Filey

North Sea

YOKE SWEATER

WITH THIS RATHER SPECIAL DESIGN I WANTED TO USE ANOTHER FORM OF SEAMLESS KNITTING
TO CREATE A GANSEY WITH A DIFFERENCE! THE PATTERNS ARE OF PARTICULAR INTEREST AND
INCLUDE REVERSE STITCH DIAMONDS AND 'HEAPIES' ALONG WITH A SCOTTISH TREE DESIGN. IN SOME
RECORDS THE 'HEAPIES' ARE TRIANGLES, OFTEN ELONGATED AND ALMOST LIKE THE FLAG DESIGN.
I PLAYED WITH THE REVERSE STOCKING (REVERSE STOCKINETTE) STITCH DIAMONDS AND 'HEAPIES'
UNTIL I FOUND THAT IT CREATED THE LOOK OF CHOPPY WATERS AND REFLECTED THE LOOK OF THE
NORTH SEA ON A WINDY DAY.

YARN

Di Gilpin Lalland DK (100% wool), 8ply/
DK light worsted, 50g (175m/191yds)

8 (9) 10 (11) balls

Shown in Furze (size S)

TENSION (GAUGE)

24 stitches and 38 rows/rounds
measure 10 x 10cm/4 x 4in over
stocking (stockinette) stitch and
Gansey stitch patterns using
3.25mm needles

NEEDLES & ACCESSORIES

1 set of 3.25mm (US 3) short double-
pointed needles and 1 set long
double-pointed needles, or circular
needles if preferred

1 set of 3.75mm (US 5) short double-
pointed needles and 1 set long
double-pointed needles, or circular
needles if preferred

A 4.5mm (US 7) straight needle

Waste yarn or stitch holders

Stitch markers

Tapestry (darning) needle

CONSTRUCTION

I have used the Fair Isle yoke sweater construction with grafted underarm sections, which is worked bottom up in the round.

PATTERN NOTES

STARTING WITH THE SLEEVES

I recommend working the sleeves first to allow you to double check your tension (gauge) over a smaller section before working the body.
This tip is great for all projects, especially if you are one of those knitters who are averse to swatching!

SLEEVES

Using 3.25mm short needles, cast on 60 (60) 72 (72) sts using a long tail cast on.

Join to start working in the round and place marker for beginning of round.

Purl 1 round.

Work rounds 1 to 33 of chart A for Sleeve cuff, repeating pattern 5 (5) 6 (6) times per round.

Change to 3.75mm needles and place a second marker after first 30 (30) 36 (36) sts.

Work 10 rounds in stocking (stockinette) stitch (knit every round).

Next round (increase): M1R, knit to marker, slip marker, M1L, knit to end. 2 sts increased.

Work 9 (9) 7 (7) rounds in stocking (stockinette) stitch.

Repeat increase round. 2 sts increased.

Repeat last 10 (10) 8 (8) rounds another 8 (10) 6 (8) times. 80 (84) 88 (92) sts.

Continue straight in stocking (stockinette) stitch until Sleeve measures 44 (46) 48 (50) cm/17¼ (18) 19 (19¾)in from cast-on edge, or desired length.

Place last 6 and first 6 sts of final round onto a stitch holder or waste yarn.

Leave remaining 68 (72) 76 (80) Sleeve sts on separate waste yarn or spare needle while you make the second. When both Sleeves are complete, work Body next.

BODY

Using 3.75mm long needles, cast on 240 (252) 264 (276) sts using a long tail cast on.

Join to start working in the round and place marker for beginning of round. If you are using double-pointed needles, slip 60 (63) 66 (69) sts onto each of four needles and work using a fifth, or if using a circular needle mark between every 60 (63) 66 (69) sts with stitch markers.

Knit 1 round.

Work rounds 1 to 44 of chart B for Body welt, repeating pattern 20 (21) 22 (23) times per round.

Continue straight in stocking (stockinette) stitch until Body measures 19 (21) 23 (25) cm/7½ (8¼) 9 (9¾)in from cast-on edge.

Change to 3.25mm long double-pointed or circular needles.

Continue straight in stocking (stockinette) stitch for another 5 (6) 7 (8)cm/2 (2¼) 2¾ (3¼)in.

Change to 3.75mm long double-pointed or circular needles.

Continue straight in stocking (stockinette) stitch until Body measures 35 (40) 42 (46) cm/13¾ (15¾) 16½ (18¼) in from cast-on edge, or desired length.

JOIN SLEEVES AND BODY FOR YOKE

Note: Before beginning this section, ensure the first 6 and last 6 sts of each Sleeve are on hold on waste yarn or a stitch holder. These will be used when grafting later and should not be knitted again.

When working this section if you are working using a circular needle you will need two colours or types of stitch markers; 4 of one type to denote raglan shaping (raglan marker) and 4 of another type to divide stitches for chart alignment (chart marker) If working using double-pointed needles, you will need 4 markers to denote raglan shaping.

Set-up round: With right side of Body facing, k54 (57) 60 (63) Body sts, leave next 12 Body sts on waste yarn for underarm, place raglan marker, k34 (36) 38 (40) Sleeve sts (these are now centre Back to centre Left Sleeve sts). If using double-pointed needles you should now have 88 (93) 98 (103) sts on your needle. Begin a new needle or, if using a circular needle, place chart marker, k34 (36) 38 (40) Sleeve sts, place raglan marker, k54 (57) 60 (63) Body sts (these are now centre Left Sleeve to centre Front sts), begin new needle or place chart marker as before, k54 (57) 60 (63) Body sts, leave next 12 Body sts on waste yarn for underarm, place raglan marker, k34 (36) 38 (40) Sleeve sts (these are now centre Front to centre Right Sleeve sts), begin new needle or place chart marker as before, k34

SIZE	TO FIT CHEST	CHEST CIRCUMFERENCE	FULL LENGTH	LENGTH TO UNDERARM	ARMHOLE DEPTH	SLEEVE LENGTH	NECK CIRCUMFERENCE
S	86cm (34in)	100cm (39½in)	54.5cm (21½in)	35cm (13¾in)	19.5cm (7¾in)	44cm (17¼in)	50cm (19¾in)
M	91cm (36in)	105cm (41¼in)	59.5cm (23½in)	40cm (15¾in)	19.5cm (7¾in)	46cm (18in)	54cm (21¼in)
L	97 (38in)	110cm (43¼in)	63cm (24¾in)	42cm (16½in)	21cm (8¼in)	48cm (19in)	52.5cm (20¾in)
XL	102cm (40in)	115cm (45¼in)	67cm (26¼in)	46cm (18¼in)	21cm (8¼in)	50cm (19¾in)	56cm (22in)

(36) 38 (40) Sleeve sts, place raglan marker, k54 (57) 60 (63) Body sts (these are now centre Right Sleeve to centre Back sts).

Rounds now begin at centre Back. If using double-pointed needles you should have 88 (93) 98 (103) sts on each needle and 4 raglan markers. If working using a circular needle you should have 4 raglan markers and 4 chart markers, with 88 (93) 98 (103) sts between chart markers. 352 (372) 392 (412) sts in total.

YOKE

Note: Yoke charts C1 and C2 do not include symbols for raglan shaping. Instructions are given below instead.

Work across charts in the following order: C1, C2, C1, C2, throughout.

Work 2 (2) 0 (0) rounds straight.

Next round (decrease): *Pattern to 4 sts before raglan marker, k2tog, k2, slip marker, k2, skp; repeat from * another 3 times. 8 sts decreased.

Work 1 round straight.

Repeat last 2 rounds another 8 (8) 9 (9) times. 280 (300) 312 (332) sts.

SIZES M AND XL ONLY

Next round (decrease): *Pattern to 4 sts before raglan marker, k2tog, k2, slip marker, pattern to next raglan marker, slip marker, k2, skp; repeat from * once more. 4 sts decreased.

ALL SIZES

280 (296) 312 (328) sts.

Continue straight in pattern until you have completed round 23 of charts C1 and C2.

Round 24 (decrease): Pattern to end, working centred double decreases where shown on chart (see *General Techniques: Centred double decrease*). 240 (256) 272 (288) sts.

Continue straight in pattern until you have completed round 30 of charts C1 and C2.

Round 31 (decrease): Pattern to end, working decreases where shown on chart as before. 192 (208) 224 (240) sts.

Round 32: Pattern to end. Charts C1 and C2 are now complete.

Begin working from chart D.

Rounds 33-40: Work straight, repeating 16-stitch pattern 12 (13) 14 (15) times per round.

Round 41 (decrease): Pattern to end, working decreases as p2tog or p2tog tbl as shown on chart. 168 (182) 196 (210) sts.

Continue as set until chart D is complete, working decreases as before on rounds 47 and 52. 120 (130) 140 (150) sts.

Work rounds 57 to 74 of chart E, repeating 10-st pattern 12 (13) 14 (15) times per round.

SIZES L AND XL ONLY

Work rounds 75 to 79 of chart E, working decreases on round 76 as shown in chart.

ALL SIZES

120 (130) 126 (135) sts.

Cast (bind) off knitwise evenly and loosely using a larger size needle.

FINISHING

Sew in any loose threads. Graft underarms (see *General Techniques: Grafting*).

If needed, lightly steam with iron held above the knitting and not on the fabric (see *General Techniques: Steam Setting*).

Yoke worked with a combination of tree and diamonds with raglan shaping

Welt in abstracted diamond/heapie patterning

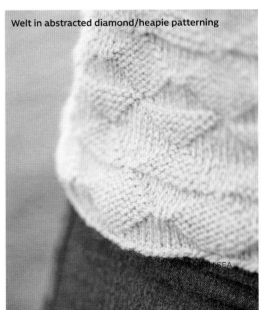

CHART A - SLEEVE

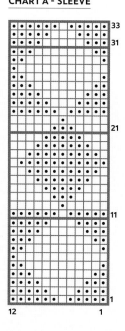

33
31

21

11

1

12   1

CHART B - WELT

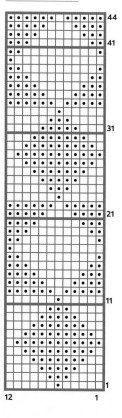

44

41

31

21

11

1

12   1

CHART D - YOKE

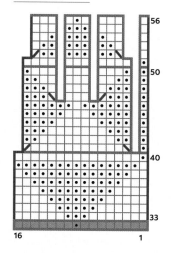

56

50

40

33

16   1

CHART F - YOKE

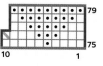

79

75

10   1

CHART E - YOKE

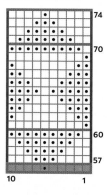

74

70

60

57

10   1

KEY

☐	RS: knit	WS: purl
▣	RS: purl	WS: knit
◩	skp	
◪	p2tog	
◪	p2tog tbl	
☐	Work sts 12 (13) 14 (15) times	
▨	Last row of previous chart	

CHART C - YOKE CHART 1

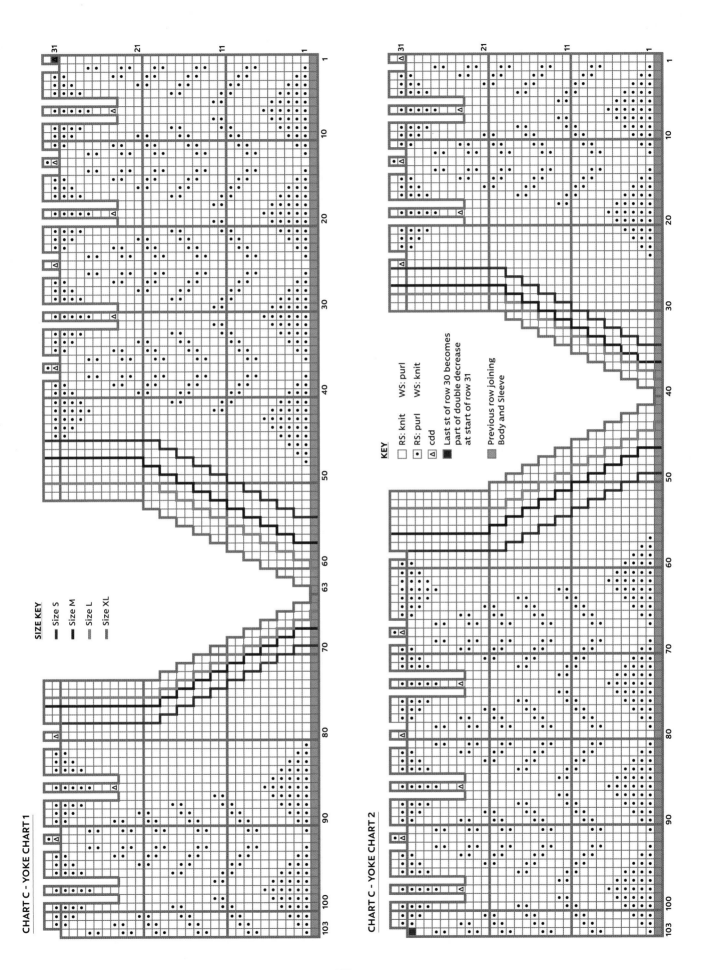

SIZE KEY
- Size S
- Size M
- Size L
- Size XL

KEY

	RS: knit	WS: purl
•	RS: purl	WS: knit
◁	cdd	
■	Last st of row 30 becomes part of double decrease at start of row 31	
▨	Previous row joining Body and Sleeve	

CHART C - YOKE CHART 2

Findhorn

GANSEY BOOT SOCKS

I REALLY WANTED TO HIGHLIGHT ONE OF MY TALENTED FRIENDS, HELEN LOCKHART, WHO LIVES OFF-GRID IN THE BEAUTIFUL ASSYNT AREA OF NORTHERN SCOTLAND. SHE IS A WONDERFUL DYER, WEAVER AND KNITTER. SHEILA AND I LOVED THIS COLOUR SHE DYED FOR US, WHICH REFLECTS THE BEAUTIFUL GORSE FLOWERS, THE FIRST TO BE SEEN IN SPRING, ON THE WILD HILLS OF THE MOORLAND. I HAVE TEAMED THIS GORGEOUS YARN UP WITH ONE OF MY FAVOURITE CABLE PATTERNS FROM FORRES, WHICH IS A VILLAGE ON THE NORTH EAST COAST OF SCOTLAND THAT I HAVE VISITED MANY TIMES.

YARN

Ripples Crafts Reliable Sock (75% wool, 25% nylon), 4ply /fingering, 100g (425m/465yds)

1 hank

Shown in Assynt Gorse

TENSION (GAUGE)

36 stitches and 48 rounds measure 10 x 10cm/4 x 4in over Forres step and cable Gansey pattern using 2.75mm needles

30 stitches and 32 rounds measure 10 x 10cm/4 x 4in over stocking (stockinette) stitch using 2.75mm needles

NEEDLES & ACCESSORIES

1 set 2.75mm (US 2) double-pointed needles, 15cm/6in long, or short circular needle

1 set 2.25mm (US 1) double-pointed needles, 15cm/6in long, or short circular needle

Cable needle

Stitch marker

Tapestry (darning) needle

PATTERN FEATURES

There is a choice of cuffs for the socks. In our samples we knitted one cuff of each design! The beautiful 'free range' cables create a lovely rippled effect, with the bars to each side. I did not extend the pattern onto the foot as I see these very much as boot socks to wear out walking on the sand dunes you find on the coast near Findhorn!

PATTERN NOTES

CUFF OPTION 1: K2, P2 RIB
(worked over 4 stitches per repeat and 16 rounds)
Rounds 1-16: K2, p2.

CUFF OPTION 2: PITTENWEEM BASKETWEAVE AND CABLE
(worked over 8 stitches per repeat and 18 rounds)
Foundation round: K4, p4.
Round 2 (increase): K4, p1, M1R, p2, M1L, p1. 10 stitches per repeat.
Rounds 3-9: K4, p2, Cable 2 Right, p2.
Round 10: P1, M1R, p2, M1L, p1, k1, k2tog, k2tog, k1.
Rounds 11-17: P2, Cable 2 Right, p2, k4.
Round 18 (decrease): K1, k2tog, k2tog, k1, k4. 8 stitches per repeat.

The special Gansey from which Sheila has worked out the pattern for the cuff option 2. Scottish Fisheries Museum Collection, ANSFM:2019.90. Photo by Di Gilpin

SIZE	One size, with adjustable foot length
FOOT LENGTH	25cm (10in), adjustable
TOP OF CUFF TO BOTTOM OF HEEL CUFF	27cm (10½in)

Cuff option 2 - work both cuffs the same or try one of each!

FORRES CABLE AND STEP CHART
(16 sts by 8 rounds Repeat)

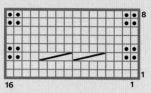

16   1

KEY

☐ RS: knit   WS: purl
▣ RS: purl   WS: knit
⬛ Cable 8 Right

CUFF

Using 2.25mm needles, cast on 64 sts using a long tail or cable cast on.

Join to start working in the round and place marker for beginning of round.

There are two choices for the rib top of these socks, the first is a very simple option and the second is a real challenge.

The second, more complex, option is the incredible pattern we found in the Scottish Fisheries Museum which uses both basketweave and cable. Sheila has worked out the pattern for this (see *Pattern Directory: Pittenweem Basketweave and Cable*).

Work 16 or 18 rounds of cuff, following your preferred option (see Pattern Notes). For our samples, we swapped options for the second sock!

LEG

Change to 2.75mm needles.

Begin working from the Forres cable and steps pattern from chart (above) or written pattern.

WRITTEN PATTERN
Round 1-2: Knit.
Round 3: P2, k2, Cable 8 Right, k2, p2.
Round 4: P2, k12, p2.
Rounds 5-6: Knit.
Rounds 7-8: P2, k12, p2.

These 8 rounds set pattern.

Complete a total of 80 rounds in pattern.

Next round (decrease): Knit to end, decreasing 4 sts evenly around. 60 sts.

HEEL FLAP (WORKED FLAT IN ROWS)
Next row (RS): K15, turn.
Next row: Slip first st, p29, turn.

Continue on these last 30 sts only, keeping remaining 30 instep sts on a spare needle.

Row 1 (RS): Slip first st, k29, turn.
Row 2: *Slip 1 purlwise wyif, p1; repeat from * to end of row.

Repeat rows 1 to 2 another 14 times, then repeat row 1 once more.

TURN HEEL

Set-up row (WS): Slip 1 purlwise, p16, p2tog, p1, turn.

Row 1 (RS): Slip first st, k5, skp, k1, turn.

Row 2: Slip first st, p6, p2tog, p1, turn.

Row 3: Slip first st, k7, skp, k1, turn.

Row 4: Slip first st, p8, p2tog, p1, turn.

Row 5: Slip first st, k9, skp, k1, turn.
Continue in this way by taking in one more st every row until all the sts of the heel flap are included, ending after a right side row. 18 heel sts remain.

SHAPE GUSSET

Set-up round: With right side facing, pick up and knit 15 sts down first side of the heel flap, place marker, knit the 30 held instep sts, place marker, pick up and knit 15 sts up second side of heel flap, k9 to take you to centre of heel. 78 sts.

Round 1 (decrease): Knit to 3 sts before first marker, k2tog, k1, slip marker, knit to next marker, slip marker, k1, skp, knit to end. 2 sts decreased.

Round 2: Knit.
Repeat these two rounds another 8 times. 60 sts.

FOOT

Knit 48 rounds, slipping markers.

To alter the size of the sock work as many rounds as you need for your length of foot, stopping about 5cm/2in short of the length you need for your foot then work the toe.

TOE

Round 1 (decrease): Knit to 3 sts before first marker, k2tog, k1, slip marker, k1, skp, knit to 3 sts before next marker, k2tog, k1, slip marker, k1, skp, knit to end. 4 sts decreased.

Round 2: Knit.
Repeat these two rounds until 24 sts are left, ending after a round 2.

Next round (partial): Knit to first marker.

FINISHING

Break yarn leaving a long tail, approximately 30cm/12in long. Graft toe sts together (see *General Techniques: Grafting*).

Make your second sock!

Ladders, cables and 2 different cuffs

Work your own sizing for foot

The Minch

FISHERFOLK'S KEP

FAIR ISLE KEPS ARE SO BEAUTIFUL AND I HAVE ALWAYS LOVED THESE LONG HATS WITH TASSELS OR POM-POMS. I STILL HAVE A RED CABLED ONE FROM WHEN I WAS FIVE! I DETERMINED TO MAKE ONE IN GANSEY PATTERNS IN TWO COLOURS TO REFLECT THE EVER-CHANGING SEA AND TOOK MY INSPIRATION FROM THE TIME I SAILED ACROSS THE MINCH IN A FRIEND'S BERMUDAN SLOOP. I WAS COOK AND BOTTLE-WASHER AND LOVED EVERY MINUTE. I WILL NEVER FORGET PUTTING DOWN ANCHOR IN REMOTE INLETS THAT PIRATES HAD INHABITED YEARS BEFORE AND SWIMMING FROM THE BOAT AT NIGHT WITH PHOSPHORESCENCE LIGHTING THE WAY IN THE DARK WATERS.

YARN

Di Gilpin Lalland DK (100% wool), 8ply/DK light worsted, 50g (175m/191yds)

1 ball in each of yarn A and yarn B

Shown with Blue Enigma as yarn A and Sea Purslane as yarn B

TENSION (GAUGE)

24 stitches and 36 rounds measure 10 x 10cm/4 x 4in over pattern using 3.5mm needles

NEEDLES & ACCESSORIES

1 set 3.5mm (US 4) double-pointed needles, 20cm/8in long, or 3.5mm (US 4) circular needle, 40cm/16in long

1 set 3.25mm (US 3) double-pointed needles, 20cm/8in long, or 3.25mm (US 3) circular needle, 40cm/16in long

Stitch markers

Tapestry (darning) needle

Note: When decreasing for the top of the kep, if you are using a 3.5mm circular needle you will need to change to 3.5mm double-pointed needles or use the Magic Loop method.

INSPIRATION

I also loved the children's books written by Arthur Ransome. *Swallows and Amazons*, the first in the series, introduces us to Nancy and Peggy who are 'pirates' with their own wee sailing boat 'Amazon'. It seems to me this kep is a pirate's kep.

PATTERN FEATURES

The first stitch pattern is my own take on the fabulous Vicar of Morwenstow's Gansey from Cornwall. I have rounded the shapes to look like the O in the OXO patterns of Fair Isle. To complement this, I used the widely-used horizontal pattern of diamonds or nets to create the X.

SIZE	One size
CIRCUMFERENCE	50cm (19¾in)
TOTAL LENGTH	35cm (13¾in) long with turn under brim

KEP

Using 3.5mm needles and yarn A, cast on 120 sts using a cable cast on.

Join to start working in the round and place marker for beginning of round.

Work in stocking (stockinette) stitch (knit every round) until brim measures 5cm/2in from cast-on edge.

Change to 3.25mm needles.

Round 1: Purl to end. This round creates the fold for the turn-under brim.

Change to 3.5mm needles.

**With yarn A, [work stitches 1-24 of row 2 of chart] 5 times.

Continue as set, working to row 66 of chart and changing yarn colour as indicated in rows 22 and 49.

Repeat rows 22-66 once more, changing colours as before.

Change to yarn B.

SHAPE TOP

With yarn B, [work row 67 of chart] 5 times. 100 stitches.

Continue as set until you have completed row 95 of chart. 20 sts.

Final round: [K2tog] 10 times. 10 sts.

Break yarn and thread through remaining sts. Pull tight to fasten.

TO MAKE UP

Sew in any loose ends.

MAKE TASSEL

Cut 2 threads of yarn A and 4 of yarn B, each approximately 40cm/15¾in long. Sew them into place on the inside at the crown of the kep. Thread through to the right side and plait (braid) to a length of 15cm/6in. Make a tassel separately with both yarns by winding them around your hand until you have a substantial amount wound. Thread the plait (braid) through at one end and tie in place. Wind thread around the tassel near to the joined section tightly. When the top of the tassel feels firm, cut through the other end to finish.

Turn the 5cm/2in stocking (stockinette) stitch brim to the inside of the kep at the false hem created by the purl round. Sew loosely but neatly in place.

Lightly steam with iron held above the knitting and not on the fabric (see *General Techniques: Steam Setting*).

Play around with colour - select yarns with higher contrast for a more striking kep

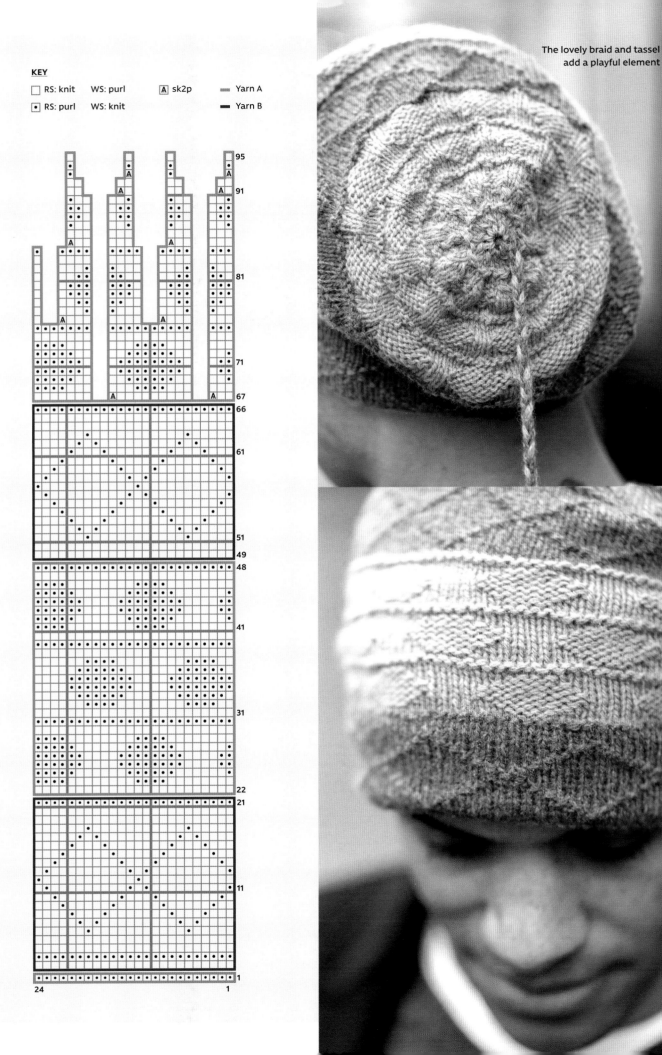

KEY

☐ RS: knit   WS: purl   Ⓐ sk2p   ▬ Yarn A

⊡ RS: purl   WS: knit   ▬ Yarn B

The lovely braid and tassel add a playful element

Cardium

GANSEY SHAWL

CONSIDERING HOW IMPORTANT THE GUSSET IS TO THE CONSTRUCTION OF THE GANSEY I DECIDED TO USE IT AS A DEVICE IN A SLIGHTLY DIFFERENT WAY TO CREATE A SHAWL COMBINED WITH ONE OF THE FEW LACE PATTERNS THAT EXIST IN GANSEY KNITTING FROM THE WESTERN ISLES IN SCOTLAND; PRINT O' THE HOOF. THE STRUCTURE OF INCREASES COMBINED WITH THE HOOF PRINT PATTERN CREATES A BEAUTIFUL HEART-SHAPED DESIGN OR CARDIUM, FROM THE GREEK FOR 'HEART', WHICH IS A FORM OF COCKLE SHELL I STILL COLLECT TODAY!

YARN

Rowan Island Blend Fine (70% wool, 15% alpaca, 15% silk), 5ply sport, 50g (165m/180yds)

2 hanks

Shown in Wedgewood

TENSION (GAUGE)

18 stitches and 24 rows measure 10 x 10cm/4 x 4in over stocking (stockinette) stitch using 5mm needles

16 stitches and 22 rows measure 10 x 10cm/4 x 4in over stocking (stockinette) stitch using 6mm needles

NEEDLES & ACCESSORIES

1 pair of 5mm (US 8) long straight needles or circular needle

1 pair 6mm (US 10) long straight needles or circular needle

1 pair 7mm (US 10½-11) long straight needles or circular needle for cast (bind) off only

INSPIRATION

I love the idea of this pattern; that it could represent the horse's hoof prints on the sand. This resonated with me having seen, as a small child, cobbles - Filey fishing boats - being taken out on a trailer drawn by horses to be launched straight into the sea from the large sandy bay.

PATTERN FEATURES

Several constants in this design give flexibility if you would like to make a longer version.

Firstly, the increases occur in 3 places only, between the two edge stitches and the main body of the shawl (at the beginning and end of rows), and either side of the centre stitch. These increases - also used in gussets - create the shape of the shawl.

Secondly, there is one main pattern, the Print O' the Hoof stitch pattern worked over 13 stitches with a purl stitch seam at each side. Once the Print O' the Hoof pattern has been 'set' it continues to the end of the shawl. When each increase section reaches 13 stitches, a new column of Print O' the Hoof starts, with a simple purl stitch between the pattern repeats.

PATTERN NOTES

CENTRED DOUBLE DECREASE

Make sure to use the centred double decrease (see *General Techniques*) which gives a lovely knit stitch running up the centre of the stitch pattern.

EDGING STITCH PATTERN

RS rows: Slip 1 knitwise, p1, pattern to last 2 stitches, p1, k1 tbl.

WS rows: Slip 1 purlwise wyif, k1, pattern to last 2 stitches, k1, p1 tbl.

SIZE	One size
LENGTH DOWN CENTRE BACK	52cm (20½in)
SIDE EDGE	62cm (24½in)
BOTTOM EDGE	72cm (28¼in)

FOUNDATION SECTION

With 5mm needles, cast on 2 sts using a long tail cast on.

Set-up row (WS): Purl.

Row 1 (RS): Knit front and back of first st, k1. 3 sts.

Row 2: Purl.

Row 3: K1, M1R, k1, M1L, k1. 5 sts.

Row 4: Purl.

Row 5: Slip 1 knitwise, p1, M1R, k1, M1L, p1, k1 tbl. 7 sts.

Row 6: Slip 1 purlwise wyif, k1, purl to last 2 sts, k1, p1 tbl.

Row 7: Slip 1 knitwise, p1, M1R, k1, M1R, k1, M1L, k1, M1L, p1, k1 tbl. 11 sts.

Row 8: Slip 1 purlwise wyif, k1, purl to last 2 sts, k1, p1 tbl.

Row 9: Work edge sts as set, M1R, knit to centre, M1R, k1, M1L, knit to last 2 sts, M1L, work edge sts as set. 2 sts increased.

Row 10: Slip 1 purlwise wyif, k1, purl to last 2 sts, k1, p1 tbl.

Keeping edge sts as set, repeat last 2 rows another 9 times ending after a wrong side row. 31 sts; 2 edge sts, 13 knit sts, 1 centre knit st, 13 knit sts, 2 edge sts.

MAIN SECTION

Row 1 (RS): Work 2 edge sts as set, M1R (to make seam st), work row 1 of chart, M1R (to make seam st), k1, M1L (to make seam st), work row 1 of chart, M1L (to make seam st), work 2 edge sts as set. 4 sts increased.

Row 2: Work 2 edge sts, k1, purl to 1 st before centre seam st, k1, p1, k1, purl to 3 sts before end, k1, work 2 edge sts.

Row 3: Work 2 edge sts, M1R, p1, work row 3 of chart, p1, M1R, k1, M1L, work row 3 of chart, p1, M1L, work 2 edge sts. 4 sts increased.

Row 4: Work 2 edge sts, p1, k1, p13, k1, p3, k1, p13, k1, p1, work 2 edge sts.

Row 5: Work 2 edge sts, M1R, k1, p1, work row 5 of chart, p1, k1, M1R, k1, M1L, k1, p1, work row 5 of chart, p1, k1, M1L, work 2 edge sts. 4 sts increased.

Row 6: Work 2 edge sts, p2, k1, p13, k1, p5, k1, p13, k1, p2, work 2 edge sts.

Row 7: Work 2 edge sts, M1R, k2, p1, work row 7 of chart, p1, k2, M1R, k1, M1L, k2, p1, work row 7 of chart, p1, k2, M1L, work 2 edge sts. 4 sts increased.

Row 8: Work 2 edge sts, p3, k1, work chart, k1, p7, k1, work chart, k1, p3, work 2 edge sts.

Row 9: Work 2 edge sts, M1R, k3, p1, work row 9 of chart, p1, k3, M1R, k1, M1L, k3, p1, work row 9 of chart, p1, k3, M1L, work 2 edge sts. 4 sts increased.

Row 10: Work 2 edge sts, p4, k1, work chart, k1, p9, k1, work chart, k1, p4, work 2 edge sts.

These last 10 rows set pattern, increases and edge sts.

Rows 11-28: Continue as set, increasing at edges and either side of centre st on right side rows, and keeping pattern correct throughout. 87 sts.

On the next row you will introduce new columns of the Print O' the Hoof chart before and after the original single column of charted sts.

Row 29 (RS): Work 2 edge sts, M1R (to make seam st), work row 1 of chart to start new column of Print O' the Hoof patterning, p1, work next row of chart as set, p1, work row 1 of chart, M1R (to make seam st), k1, M1L (to make seam st), work row 1 of chart, p1, work next row of chart as set, p1, work row 1 of chart, M1L (to make seam st), work 2 edge sts. 4 sts increased.

Row 30: Work 2 edge sts, k1, p13, k1, p13, k1, p13, k1, p1, k1, p13, k1, p13, k1, p13, k1, work 2 edge sts.

Continue increasing at the shawl edges and in the centre, working the Print O' the Hoof pattern as each new section reaches 13 sts, with a purl seam st between.

When you have completed 90 rows, change to 6mm needles.

Continue increasing and adding repeats as set until you have completed 10 pattern repeats in the centre column of each side of the shawl. This should be another 10 rows after changing to 6mm needles.

You should have the following number of Print O' the Hoof repeats in each column: 1, 4, 7, 10, 7, 4, 1, centre st, 1, 4, 7, 10, 7, 4, 1.

Cast (bind) off knitwise on the right side using 7mm needles.

Alternatively, if you want to carry on to make a much larger shawl, simply continue in the sequence as set, remembering that this may require more yarn.

KEY

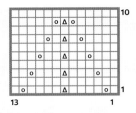

☐ RS: knit   WS: purl

△ cdd

○ yarnover

FINISHING

When the cast (bind) off is complete, steam shawl holding iron over the sts on the wrong side and ease out to measurements (see *General Techniques: Steam Setting*).

Put more pressure on the cast-off (bound-off) sts on the right side of the shawl, allowing them to sit flat so that the wavy edge can be clearly seen.

Print o'the Hoof pattern in lace

Sea Biscuit

CARDIGAN

SHEILA AND I BOTH WANTED TO CREATE A GANSEY-STYLE CARDIGAN THAT ALLOWED THE KNITTER TO PLAY AND EXPLORE SOME OF THE FABULOUS PATTERNS IN THE PATTERN DIRECTORY OF THIS BOOK. THE GRID REMINDED ME OF THE SEA BISCUITS, OR 'HARD TACK', TAKEN ON BOARD SHIPS FOR LONG JOURNEYS. OFTEN MADE IN A SQUARE FROM SIMPLY FLOUR, WATER AND SALT, THEY WERE SOMETIMES MARKED IN A GRID TO DIVIDE UP AND SHARE. IT IS ALSO THE NAME OF A FASCINATING TYPE OF SEA URCHIN WITH A BEAUTIFULLY PATTERNED SHELL. THIS CARDIGAN IS A SPACE TO EXPERIMENT AND HAVE FUN. TO CREATE YOUR VERY OWN DESIGN!

YARN

Di Gilpin Lalland DK (100% wool), 8ply/
DK light worsted, 50g (175m/191yds)

7 (8) 10 balls

Shown in Sea Purslane (size M)

TENSION (GAUGE)

22 stitches and 36 rows/rounds
measure 10 x 10cm/4 x 4in over
stocking (stockinette) stitch using
3.75mm needles

NEEDLES & ACCESSORIES

1 pair of 3.25mm (US 3) long straight
needles or long circular needle for body

1 set of 3.25mm (US 3) double-pointed
needles or short circular needle
for sleeves

1 pair of 3.75mm (US 5) long straight
needles or long circular needle for body

1 set of 3.75mm (US 5) double-pointed
needles or short circular needle
for sleeves

Waste yarn or stitch holders

Tapestry (darning) needle

CONSTRUCTION

This cardigan is worked seamlessly, with two neat little gussets, as befits a Gansey-inspired garment. Back and both fronts are worked in one piece up to the armholes, where they split into three separate pieces. Each front has an integral knitted edge and the fronts are joined to the back using shoulder straps, which are grafted on. The sleeves are picked up and worked downwards from shoulder to cuff in the round, as all Ganseys should be.

MAKE YOUR OWN VERSION

We created a grid based on the Cornish Steps design which gives a great base to add to. We have chosen small diamonds but you could also insert hearts, heapies or even your own initials or letters to make a word. There are also some excellent Gansey alphabets in the books you will find in the bibliography. Enjoy - and we look forward to seeing the end results!

PATTERN NOTES

EDGING STITCHES

When working Front edgings, they are always worked as:

RS rows: Slip 1 knitwise, p1, pattern as given to last 2 stitches, p1, k1 tbl.

WS rows: Slip 1 purlwise wyif, k1, pattern as given to last 2 stitches, k1, p1 tbl.

These 4 stitches are uncharted.

Note: When working this integrated edging, knit with extreme care to ensure the slipped twisted stitches are firm and neat throughout, and also make sure to keep the cast (bind) offs for all edges tight and steady.

BODY

Using 3.25mm long straight needles or circular needle, cast on 245 (293) 341 sts using long tail cast on.

Row 1 (WS): Slip 1 purlwise wyif, knit to last st, p1 tbl.

Row 2 (RS): Slip 1 knitwise, p1, repeat sts 1-24 of row 2 of chart A 10 (12) 14 times, work st 1 of chart A once more, p1, k1 tbl.

Row 3 (WS): Slip 1 purlwise wyif, k1, work st 1 of row 3 of chart A once, repeat sts 24-1 of row 3 of chart A 10 (12) 14 times, k1, p1 tbl.

Rows 2 and 3 set edge sts and pattern repeat.

Continue in pattern as set until row 12 of chart A is complete.

Change to 3.75mm long straight needles or circular needle.

Continue in pattern as set until you have completed row 96 of chart A.

SIZE L ONLY

Repeat rows 25 to 48 of Chart A once more.

ALL SIZES
INCREASE FOR GUSSETS

Gussets are worked in stocking (stockinette) stitch with a centre seam st in garter stitch. This section is worked over 12 rows of pattern, working rows 25 (25) 49 to 36 (36) 60 of chart A, while increasing for gussets at the same time as follows:

Next row (WS): Keeping pattern and edge sts correct, work as row 25 (25) 49.

Next row (RS): Working as row 26 (26) 50, work 62 (74) 86 sts, M1R, k1, M1L, work 119 (143) 167 sts, M1R, k1, M1L, work 62 (74) 86 sts to end.

Next row: Working as row 27 (27) 51, work 63 (75) 87 sts, k1 (seam st), work 121 (145) 169 sts, k1 (seam st), work 63 (75) 87 sts to end.

Next row: Working as row 28 (28) 52, work 62 (74) 86 sts, M1R, k3, M1L, work 119 (143) 167 sts, M1R, k3, M1L, work 62 (74) 86 sts to end.

Continue as set for another 8 rows, increasing either side of the gusset on every right side row, ending after a right side row. When increasing, keep the gusset in stocking (stockinette) stitch except the centre seam st, which should be knitted every row.

You should have increased a total of 6 times, with 13 sts now for each gusset and a total of 269 (317) 365 sts.

Next row (WS): Keeping pattern and edge sts correct, *work as row 37 (37) 61 to edge of gusset, p6, k1, p6; repeat from * once more, pattern to end..

DIVIDE FOR FRONTS AND BACK

Next row (RS): Keeping pattern and edge sts correct, *work as row 38 (38) 62 to edge of gusset, k1, slip next 11 sts from gusset onto waste yarn, k1; repeat from * once more, pattern to end.

Note: When working separately for the Fronts and Back, work rows 39 (39) 63 to 84 (84) 96, and then (for size L only), rows - (-) 25 to - (-) 48 of chart A, keeping Front edge sts as set.

LEFT FRONT

Turn and continue on group of last 63 (75) 87 sts for Left Front, leaving remaining sts on a spare needle or waste yarn. The Front edge sts are worked at the end of a right side row and the beginning of a wrong side row. The single st at the gusset edge is not patterned but continues in stocking (stockinette) stitch and is the armhole edge st for Back and Fronts, and is also not shown on chart A.

Work Left Front until row 84 (84) 96 of chart A has been completed.

SIZE L ONLY

Work rows 25 to 48 of chart A once more.**

SIZE	TO FIT CHEST	BACK WIDTH	LENGTH TO SIDE SHOULDER	LENGTH TO BEGINNING OF GUSSET SHAPING	ARMHOLE DEPTH INCLUDING GUSSET DEPTH	SLEEVE LENGTH	BACK NECK WIDTH
S	81-97cm (32-38in)	54cm (24¼in)	52cm (20½in)	27cm (10½in)	25cm (10in)	44.5cm (17½in)	20.5cm (8in)
M	102-117cm (40-46in)	65cm (25½in)	52cm (20½in)	27cm (10½in)	25cm (10in)	44.5cm (17½in)	31.5cm (12½in)
L	122-137cm (48-54in)	76cm (30in)	62cm (24¼in)	33cm (13in)	28.5cm (11¼in)	49.5cm (19½in)	31.5cm (12½in)

ALL SIZES
SHAPE NECK AND SHOULDERS

Keeping pattern alignment as before, work rows 1 to 13 of chart B.

Row 14 (RS): K1, working row 14 of chart B, pattern across 37 (37) 49 sts, k to end.

Row 15 (WS): Using a 3.25mm straight needle to give a firmer edge, cast (bind) off 24 (36) 36 sts purlwise (first neck edge st is now on right needle), continue using 3.75mm needle, k1 (second neck edge st), pattern to last st, p1.

Continue straight on remaining sts in pattern.

Work rows 16 to 24 of chart B.

Work rows 1 to 24 of chart B once more.

Leave sts on spare needle or waste yarn, ready for grafting shoulder.

RIGHT FRONT

With wrong side facing, rejoin yarn to Right Front at gusset edge.

Work as for Left Front, to **, noting that the Front edge sts are worked at the end of a wrong side row and the beginning of a right side row.

ALL SIZES
SHAPE NECK AND SHOULDERS

Keeping pattern alignment as before, work rows 1 to 13 of chart B.

Row 14 (RS): Using a 3.25mm straight needle to give a firmer edge, cast (bind) off 24 (36) 36 sts knitwise (first neck edge st is now on right needle), continue using 3.75mm needle, p1 (second neck edge st), pattern to last st, k1.

Continue straight on remaining sts in pattern.

Work rows 15 to 24 of chart B.

Work rows 1 to 24 of chart B once more.

Leave sts on spare needle or waste yarn, ready for grafting shoulder.

BACK

Rejoin yarn to centre 121 (145) 169 sts. The first and last sts are not charted; work these as stocking (stockinette) stitch to create a flat armhole edge.

Note that the first and last pattern sts are now omitted, so the pattern starts on st 2 of the chart at the beginning of row only. All of the grids should stay in line as a result.

Work rows 39 (39) 63 to 84 (84) 96 of chart A and then (for size L only), rows - (-) 25 to - (-) 48 of chart A again.

Work rows 1 to 12 of chart B.

Beautiful diamond pattern at cuff

Now transfer 38 (38) 50 sts from each end of the row onto waste yarn, ready to be grafted to the Front shoulder straps.

Rejoin yarn to remaining centre 45 (69) 69 sts with wrong side facing.

Work as for row 13 of chart B, keeping pattern correct.

Change to 3.25mm needles.

Cast (bind) off knitwise.

GRAFTING

Graft the Front shoulder straps to the Back shoulder segments using a purl grafting stitch (see *General Techniques: Grafting*). This should keep the pattern flowing without disruption.

SLEEVES

The Sleeves are formed by picking up a total of 107 (107) 119 sts around the Back and Front armholes and completing the gussets at the same time.

Note: When working chart B across Sleeve sts, omit the first st of each chart row on the first chart repeat.

Round 1: Using 3.75mm double-pointed needles or a short circular needle, and with right side facing, beginning at the gusset seam st, k6 across first side of gusset, then pick up and knit 54 (54) 60 sts evenly up armhole edge to top shoulder, 53 (53) 59 sts down armhole edge to remaining gusset sts, k5 across remaining gusset sts and place marker for beginning of round. 118 (118) 130 sts.

Round 2: K4, k2tog, work row 2 of chart B to last 5 sts, skp, k3. 116 (116) 128 sts; 107 (107) 119 Sleeve sts and 9 sts for gusset.

Round 3: P1, k4, work row 3 of chart B to last 4 sts, k4.

Round 4: K3, k2tog, work row 4 of chart B to last 4 sts, skp, k2. 114 (114) 126 sts; 107 (107) 119 Sleeve sts and 7 sts for gusset.

Round 5: P1, k3, work row 5 of chart B to last 3 sts, k3.

Round 6: K2, k2tog, work row 6 of chart B to last 3 sts, skp, k1. 112 (112) 124 sts; 107 (107) 119 Sleeve sts and 5 sts for gusset.

Round 7: P1, k2, work row 7 of chart B to last 2 sts, k2.

Round 8: K1, k2tog, work row 8 of chart B to last 2 sts, skp 110 (110) 122 sts; 107 (107) 119 Sleeve sts and 3 sts for gusset.

Round 9: P1, k1, work row 9 of chart B to last st, ending round here (1 st of round remains).

Round 10: Slip 1 knitwise, k2tog, pass slipped st over, work row 10 of chart B to end of round. 108 (108) 120 sts; 107 (107) 119 Sleeve sts and 1 seam st.

Now continue working straight until you have completed row 24 of chart B, keeping seam st in garter stitch (purl 1 round, knit 1 round) throughout.

SHAPE SLEEVES

Round 1: P1 (seam st), k1, skp, k to last 3 sts of round, k2tog, k1. 2 sts decreased.

Round 2: Knit.

Round 3: P1, knit to end of round.

Round 4: Knit.

Repeat rounds 1 to 4 until 60 (60) 72 sts remain.

Work straight in stocking (stockinette) stitch with garter seam st until Sleeve measures 39 (39) 44cm/15¼ (15¼) 17¼in from picked-up edge.

Change to 3.25mm double-pointed needles or short circular needle.

Work rows 1 to 13 of chart B.

Cast (bind) off using preferred method.

The sample used the following method: *K2tog, then transfer resulting st back to left needle, k2tog; repeat from * to end. Fasten off remaining st.

Work second Sleeve to match the first.

FINISHING

Sew in any loose threads.

Lightly steam with iron held above the knitting and not on the fabric (see *General Techniques: Steam Setting*).

CHART A

CHART B

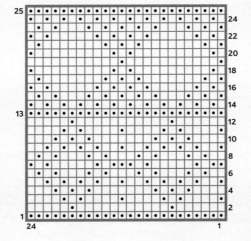

You can use a lovely brooch or pin at the neck edge for a personal touch

KEY

- ☐ RS: knit   WS: purl
- ⊡ RS: purl   WS: knit
- ▬ Repeat for size L only

The Calypso

SUMMER VEST

I SPENT MANY HAPPY DAYS SAILING IN THE WESTERN ISLES WHEN I LIVED ON THE ISLE OF SKYE. CALYPSO WAS THE BEAUTIFUL BOAT OWNED BY TIM, THE SKIPPER WHO USED TO INVITE US AT THE WEEKEND TO SAIL OVER THE MINCH TO EXPLORE THE BEAUTIFUL COASTLINE OF THE OUTER HEBRIDES. THIS DESIGN IS WITH THANKS TO TIM AND HIS LOVELY FAMILY FOR LETTING ME CREW THE BOAT AND FOR LEAVING SUCH AMAZING MEMORIES OF SUNNY HEBRIDEAN DAYS!

YARN
Quince & Co. Sparrow (100% organic linen), 4ply/fingering, 50g (154m/168yds)

4 (5) 5 hanks

Shown in shade Citron (size Small)

TENSION (GAUGE)
30 stitches and 34 rows/rounds measure 10 x 10cm/4 x 4in over pattern using 3mm needles

NEEDLES & ACCESSORIES
1 set of 3mm (US 2-3) double-pointed needles or long circular needle for body

1 pair of 3mm (US 2-3) straight needles for front and back sections worked straight after armhole divide

1 pair of 2.75mm (US 2) straight needles for front and back sections worked straight after armhole divide

Cable needle

Stitch markers

Tapestry (darning) needle

LIFE ABOARD THE CALYPSO

The Calypso would land on small islands, now uninhabited save for the amazing birds that took sanctuary there. Porpoise would leap in the bow waves of the boat and we saw orca pods gliding through the Minch. We fished for mackerel and I would throw the fish in the pan and cook them straight away for supper.

PATTERN FEATURES

This summer garment features the Eriskay Star design and Print O' the Hoof lace pattern, alongside ropes, a fabulous seeding pattern and the iconic Pittenweem Tree design, unique to the east coast of Scotland. The tree seems to be a visual pun to me, so I have knitted it first as a tree and then upside down as a herringbone! The linen works beautifully with the lace and shows how Gansey stitch patterns can be worked in many different fibres to great effect.

BODY

Using 3mm needles, cast on 240 (272) 304 sts, using your favourite method.

Join to start working in the round and place marker for beginning of round.

Place a second marker after first 120 (136) 152 sts.

WELT

Set-up round: *Work row 1 of Welt chart for your size to marker, slip marker; repeat from * once more.

Note: *The final st before each marker is a seam st and is worked in stocking (stockinette) stitch throughout.*

Continue in Welt pattern as set until piece measures 4 (6.5) 9cm/1⅝ (2½) 3½in from cast-on edge.

MAIN PATTERN

Continue in seeding pattern as previously set from Welt chart for your size at either side of the markers and in between charts as follows:

Set-up round: *Work 5 (9) 13 sts in seeding pattern as set, work row 1 of chart 1, work 7 (11) 15 sts in seeding pattern as set, work row 1 of chart 2, work 7 (11) 15 sts in seeding pattern as set, work row 1 of chart 1, work 6 (10) 14 sts in seeding pattern as set (including seam st), slip marker; repeat from * once more.

Continue in pattern as set until you have worked a total of 60 rounds in Main Pattern. You should have worked 5 full repeats of chart 1.

FRONT

DIVIDE FOR FRONT AND BACK

Note: *Front and Back are now worked separately, back and forth in rows.*

*** Next row (RS): Cast (bind) off 5 (9) 13 sts (side seed sts), pattern as set to side marker, turn. Chart 2 is now complete.

Note: *From next row onwards, you will work rows 38 to 1 of chart 2 in **reverse** order to create the centre herringbone pattern. When these rows of chart 2 are complete, work rows 39 to 61 of chart 2 in order once more.*

Next row (WS): Cast (bind) off 6 (10) 14 sts (side seed sts and seam st), pattern until you have 107 (115) 123 sts on right needle, k1, p1 tbl.

Cont on these 109 (117) 125 sts for Front and leave remaining 120 (136) 152 sts on a spare needle for Back.

From now on the first and last cable panels of each row (in chart 1) should be worked in stocking (stockinette) stitch until they have been decreased away by armhole shaping.

From beginning of armhole shaping and thereafter, work 2 edge sts at beginning and end of each row as follows:

EDGING STITCHES

RS rows: Slip 1 knitwise, p1, pattern as given to last 2 sts, p1, k1 tbl.

WS rows: Slip 1 purlwise wyif, k1, pattern as given to last 2 sts, k1, p1 tbl.

These 4 sts are not included in the charts.

SHAPE ARMHOLES

Next row (RS decrease): Work 2 edge sts, skp, pattern to last 4 sts, k2tog, work 2 edge sts. 2 sts decreased.

Next row (WS): Work 2 edge sts, pattern to last 2 sts, work 2 edge sts.

Repeat last 2 rows another 7 times. 93 (101) 109 sts.

Continue straight in pattern and edging sts as set until you have completed row 61 of chart 2 again, ending after a wrong side row.

DIVIDE FOR RIGHT AND LEFT NECK

Change to 2.75mm needles.

Next row (RS): Work 2 edge sts, pattern 43 (47) 51 sts, cast (bind) off next 3 sts (central 3 sts above the star design), pattern to last 2 sts, work 2 edge sts. 45 (49) 53 sts remain per side.

Turn and work on first set of 45 (49) 53 sts only.

SIZE	TO FIT CHEST	HEM CIRCUMFERENCE	LENGTH TO UNDERARM	ARMHOLE DEPTH	LENGTH TO SIDE SHOULDER
S	76-81cm (30-32in)	80cm (31½in)	21.5cm (8½in)	28.5cm (11¼in)	50cm (19¾in)
M	86-91cm (34-36in)	90.5cm (35¾in)	24cm (9½in)	28.5cm (11¼in)	52.5cm (20¾in)
L	97-102cm (38-40in)	101cm (39¾in)	26.5cm (10½in)	28.5cm (11¼in)	55cm (21¾in)

SHAPE FIRST SIDE NECK

Next row (WS): Work 2 edge sts, pattern 41 (45) 49 sts, work 2 edge sts.

This row sets edge sts at armhole and neck edges. Continue in pattern as set, while shaping neck as follows:

Next row (RS decrease): Work 2 edge sts, skp, pattern to last 2 sts, work 2 edge sts. 1 st decreased.

Work 1 row straight.

**Repeat last 2 rows another 15 times. 29 (33) 37 sts.

Continue straight until work measures 50 (52.5) 55cm/19¾ (20¾) 21¾in from cast-on edge, ending after a wrong side row. If worked to correct tension (gauge) you should not need to work further rows.

Set sts aside on waste yarn.

SHAPE SECOND SIDE NECK

With wrong side facing, rejoin yarn to neck edge of remaining neck sts.

Next row (WS): Work 2 edge sts, pattern 41 (45) 49 sts, work 2 edge sts.

This row sets edge sts at armhole and neck edges. Continue in pattern as set, while shaping neck as follows:

Next row (RS decrease): Work 2 edge sts, pattern to last 4 sts, k2tog, work 2 edge sts. 1 st decreased.

Work 1 row straight.

Work as for first side neck from ** to end, setting sts aside on waste yarn.

BACK

Rejoin yarn to remaining 120 (136) 152 sts. Work as for Front from *** to end.

FINISHING

With right sides together, join shoulders using the 3-needle cast (bind) off method (see *General Techniques*).

Sew in any loose threads.

Lightly steam with iron held above the knitting and not on the fabric (see *General Techniques: Steam Setting*).

KEY

☐	RS: knit	WS: purl
•	RS: purl	WS: knit
⟋	Cable 6 Left	
⟍	Cable 6 Right	
O	yarnover	
A	sk2p	
☐	Repeat	
☐	Seam st	

WELT CHART - SIZE S

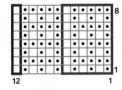

12   1

WELT CHART - SIZE M

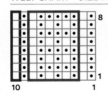

10   1

WELT CHART - SIZE L

14   1

CHART 1

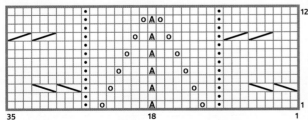

35   18   1

CHART 2

25   13   1

GENERAL TECHNIQUES

HOW TO READ CHARTS

When working from charts each square represents a stitch. When working in rows, read right side (odd) rows of the chart from right to left and wrong side (even) rows from left to right. When working in the round, read all rows of the chart from right to left. Sections between coloured repeat lines should be repeated the indicated number of times before continuing with the rest of the stitches for that row of the chart. If the number of repeats is not given, repeat the section between the coloured lines until you do not have enough stitches to work another repeat, then work any stitches that come after those between the coloured lines.

STEAM SETTING YOUR FINISHED PROJECT

Always check the ball band for any yarn care instructions. For the Gansey projects we don't recommend wet blocking as it would damage the stitch definition of the Gansey. Steaming and pressing down lightly with the fingertips is the best method for settling out the stitches in, for example, the *Cardium Gansey Shawl*, or the edge stitches of **Sea Biscuit Cardigan** (see *Projects*).

Work from the wrong side of the fabric and carefully hold the steam iron above the stitches needing attention from about 5cm/2in. Keeping your hands away from the hot steam, use your fingertips to gently press down on the edges or stitches to guide them into place.

LONG TAIL CAST ON

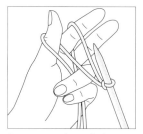 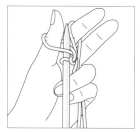  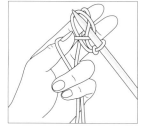

Step one: Make a slip knot on right needle, making sure yarn tail is long enough for cast-on edge. Keep the working yarn attached to the ball in the front (thumb side).

Step two: Insert your left thumb and left index finger between the yarn tail and the working yarn, holding both strands with remaining left fingers.

Step three: Insert needle under the strand wrapped around left thumb, then go up and over the strand wrapped around left index finger to scoop it onto the needle tip.

Step four: Bring loop on tip out through thumb loop, then drop loop on thumb and pull yarn to tighten stitch on right needle. **Repeat** steps two to four as needed.

CABLE CAST ON

  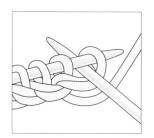 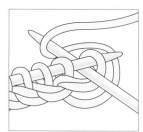

Step one: Make a slip knot on left needle as your first stitch.

Step two: Knit into this stitch with right needle, pulling loop through and place loop as a new stitch onto left needle (two stitches cast on).

Step three: Insert right needle between first two stitches on left needle.

Step four: Wrap yarn around tip as if to knit, pull loop through, place as new stitch onto left needle. **Repeat** steps three to four as needed.

CENTRED DOUBLE DECREASE (CDD)

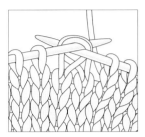

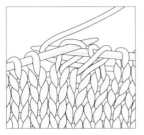

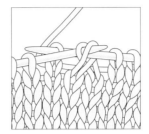

Step one: Working to one full stitch before central stitch, slip next 2 stitches on left needle together knitwise.

Step two: Knit 1 stitch.

Step three: Pass the 2 slipped stitches over.

LEFT-LEANING DOUBLE DECREASE (SK2P)

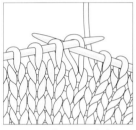

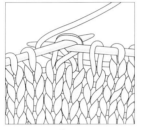

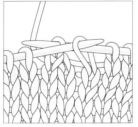

Step one: Slip next stitch on left needle.

Step two: Knit next two stitches on left needle together.

Step three: Pass the slipped stitch over.

MOCK CABLE

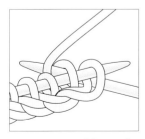

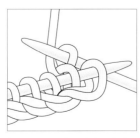

Step one: Insert right needle through back loop of second stitch on left needle.

Step two: Make a knit stitch but leave original stitch on left needle.

Step three: Bring right needle to front of work and insert in first stitch on left needle and knit the stitch as normal.

Step four: Allow both stitches to drop from left needle together.

BASIC CAST (BIND) OFF

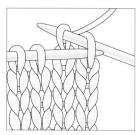 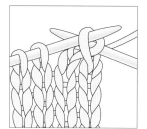 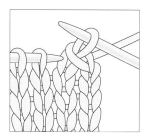

Step one: With two stitches on right needle, insert left needle tip into first stitch on right needle.

Step two: Pass this stitch over second stitch and off needle.

Step three: One stitch is now cast (bind) off. Work next stitch and repeat from step one until last stitch remains on right needle. Break yarn, pull tail through last stitch and sew end in.

3-NEEDLE CAST (BIND) OFF

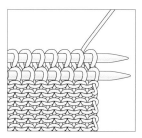 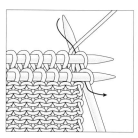 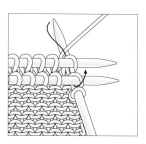 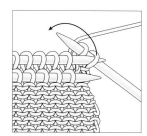

Step one: Arrange both pieces with wrong sides facing out (for internal seam) or with right sides facing out (for external seam).

Step two: Hold needles parallel and slip a third (working) needle into first stitch on each of the two needles and k2tog.

Step three: Knit together the new first stitch on both parallel needles in the same way. There will be two stitches on working needle.

Step four: Pass first stitch on working needle over second and off the needle to cast (bind) off.
Repeat steps three to four until one stitch remains on working needle. Break yarn and pull tail through last stitch and sew end in.

GRAFTING (KITCHENER STITCH)

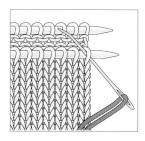 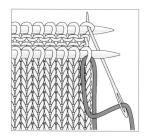 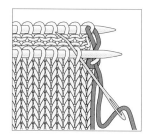 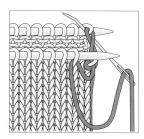

Step one: Arrange remaining stitches evenly on two double-pointed needles held parallel with right side facing and both tips to the right. Thread tapestry needle with attached yarn.

Step two: Insert tapestry needle purlwise through first stitch on front needle, leaving stitch on needle, then insert tapestry needle knitwise through first stitch on back needle, leaving stitch on needle.

Step three: Insert knitwise through first stitch on front needle, then purlwise through second stitch and allow only first stitch to drop.

Step four: Insert purlwise through first stitch on back needle, then knitwise through second stitch and allow only first stitch to drop.
Repeat steps three to four until all stitches are grafted.

ABBREVIATIONS

Cable 2 Left: Put 1 stitch from left needle to cable needle and hold at front of the work. Knit the next 1 stitch on left needle and then knit 1 stitch from cable needle

Cable 2 Right: Put 1 stitch from left needle to cable needle and hold at back of the work. Knit the next 1 stitch on left needle and then knit 1 stitch from cable needle

Cable 4 Left: Put 2 stitches from left needle to cable needle and hold at front of the work. Knit the next 2 stitches on left needle and then knit 2 stitches from cable needle

Cable 6 Left: Put 3 stitches from left needle to cable needle and hold at front of the work. Knit the next 3 stitches on left needle and then knit 3 stitches from cable needle

Cable 6 Right: Put 3 stitches from left needle to cable needle and hold at back of the work. Knit the next 3 stitches on left needle and then knit 3 stitches from cable needle

Cable 8 Left: Put 4 stitches from left needle to cable needle and hold at front of the work. Knit the next 4 stitches on left needle and then knit 4 stitches from cable needle

Cable 8 Right: Put 4 stitches from left needle to cable needle and hold at back of the work. Knit the next 4 stitches on left needle and then knit 4 stitches from cable needle

Cable 10 Left: Put 5 stitches from left needle to cable needle and hold at front of the work. Knit the next 5 stitches on left needle and then knit 5 stitches from cable needle

Cable 12 Right: Put 6 stitches from left needle to cable needle and hold at back of the work. Knit the next 6 stitches on left needle and then knit 6 stitches from cable needle

cdd: centred double decrease (see *General Techniques: Centred double decrease*)

corn stitch: yarnover, knit 2 stitches, pass yarnover loop over those 2 stitches

RS: knit **WS:** purl

k2tog: make a right-leaning decrease (see *Gansey Techniques: Working right- and left-leaning decreases*)

M1L: make a left-leaning increase (see *Gansey Techniques: Working right- and left-leaning increases*)

M1R: make a right-leaning increase (see *Gansey Techniques: Working right- and left-leaning increases*)

Mock Cable: left twist false cable (see *General Techniques: Mock Cable*)

RS: purl **WS:** knit

p2tog: make a right-leaning decrease by purling 2 stitches together

p2tog tbl: make a left-leaning decrease by purling 2 stitches together through the back loops

RS: right side

sk2p: left-leaning double decrease (see *General Techniques: Left-leaning Double Decrease*)

skp: make a left-leaning decrease (see *Gansey Techniques: Working right- and left-leaning decreases*)

slip stitch: move stitch from left needle to right needle without twisting and keep yarn held to wrong side

st(s): stitch(es)

tbl: through the back loop

WS: wrong side

wyib: with yarn in back

wyif: with yarn in front

yarnover: bring yarn over needle

ABOUT THE AUTHORS

Sheila Greenwell

I come from a Scottish knitwear town and from a family closely connected to spinning and wool, so I could knit before I went to primary school. Looking at old handwritten notes from Gansey knitters reminds me strongly of how I knitted as a learner without the benefit of printed patterns. I met Di 10 years ago, having retired after 30 years of teaching, and now I am lucky enough to share both teaching and knitting with her. The Gansey story always captivates our audiences around the world and it has been a great privilege to work with Di on this book.

Di Gilpin

In 1983, I took a year off from teaching History to travel, arriving on the Isle of Skye with little more than a rucksack containing a tent, some wool and knitting needles. I ended up spending 18 years on the island, inspired by nature, landscape and sea. I worked on my own knitting skills, experimenting with different processes, styles and stitches.

Now based at Comielaw Farm on the Balcaskie Estate in Fife, I create wool ranges, including an organic wool/cashmere in collaboration with Uist Wool. Sheila and I work together designing knitting patterns, garments for different fashion clients, teaching and workshops. I helped develop the Moray Firth Partnership Gansey Project and, along with Sheila, contribute to the steering committee for the 'Knitting the Herring' Project with the Scottish Fisheries Museum. I now have a company with Sheila and a wonderful team working from the studio. Our brand involves collaborations with designers including Graeme Black, Paul Hardy, Nike, La Fetiche and Connolly England. Slow Fashion, ethical and sustainable production are our ethos.
Balvenie Masters of Craft Textile Award, 2005 and 2012.
Fletcher of Saltoun Award from the Saltire Society, 2019.

ACKNOWLEDGEMENTS

We would like to dedicate this book to all the amazing Gansey knitters whose work has inspired us over the years.

With thanks to everyone involved in 'Knitting the Herring'. Federica Papiccio for the hours spent with her recording details of each Gansey. Matthew Topsfield for all the excellent work he is doing with Eriskay Gansey research and knitting. Jen Gordon from the Museum, who has researched a great deal of the Textile Collection in Anstruther. Stephanie Hoyle and Kathryn Logan from the Moray Firth Gansey project for creating a wonderful Gansey legacy to be taken forward with the Scottish Fisheries Museum. Linda Fitzpatrick for all her help with the Museum archives. Maureen Malecki and Sandra Buttercase for knitting some of the beautiful final pieces in the book. Big thanks to our very own Knitting Club for all the support over this past year, we love you all!

Thanks to Martin Warren, whose work on the Sheringham Ganseys has been invaluable. Anji Hancock has been incredible too in sharing all the knowledge she has gleaned about her grandmother Isabella, whose notes and patterns we include in the history chapter. Thanks to Oisin Davis Lyons, my stepson, who modelled for us in Bristol and whose artwork appears in the book. www.oshii.uk. Thanks to Rachel Kiley, Funso Foluso-Henry, Claire Rammelkamp, Hudson and Adeline Rowntree for being wonderful models. A special thanks to Sarah Rowntree for art direction and design, along with photographer Jason Jenkins and editor Jessica Cropper. Thanks to Sarah Callard for believing in the book from the very first conversation last year. Sheila and I are so thrilled with all the work our publishers David & Charles have put into this book. Tricia Gilbert has been fabulous to work with too and we thank you so much!

This has been a fascinating research project that Sheila and I have loved. We would both like to thank Colm and Howard and our boys for their personal and professional support and understanding. I would like to say the biggest thank you to Sheila for keeping me on the right path in this journey through the Gansey story.

BIBLIOGRAPHY

For those of you new to the Gansey, or already in love with this incredible form of knitting, I have made a bibliography of my favourite Gansey books, articles and websites.

Sources of particular note

The Scottish Fisheries Museum Gansey Project 'Knitting the Herring' has a wonderful archive of Ganseys from the Moray Firth Project and the East Neuk of Fife. Knit a herring for the project! *www.scottishgansey.org.uk*

Michael Pearson's *Traditional Knitting. Aran, Fair Isle and Fisher Ganseys*. Dover Publications, Inc, Minneola, New York, 1985. ISBN 0004120566
A really sensitive and wonderful book with in-depth research from a time when Gansey knitters could still be interviewed.

Gladys Thompson. *Patterns for Guernseys, Jerseys & Arans. Fishermen's Sweaters from the British Isles*. Dover Publications, 2000. ISBN 0486227030
The book which started my research as a child. A must have for Gansey lovers.

Beth Brown-Reinsel. *Knitting Ganseys: Techniques and Patterns for Traditional Sweaters*, Revised and Updated. Interweave Press, 2018. ISBN 9781632506160
A fabulous book with some beautiful traditional designs.

Other books

Rae Compton. *The Complete Book of Traditional Guernsey and Jersey Knitting*. Batsford Ltd, London, 1984. ISBN 0713441259

Sabine Dominick. *Cables, Diamonds & Herringbone: Secrets of Knitting Traditional Fishermen's Sweaters*. Camden, 2007. ISBN 9780892726882

Marie Hartley and Joan Ingilby. *The Old Hand-Knitters of the Dales*. Cooperative Press, additional text Penelope Hemingway ©2014, text of original book ©1951. ISBN 9781937513269

Michael Harvey & Rae Compton. *Fishermen Knitting*. Shire Publications, London, 1978. ISBN 0852634218

Penelope Lister Hemingway. *River Ganseys: Strikin' t'loop, Swaving, and Other Yorkshire Knitting Curiosities Revived from the Archives*. Cooperative Press, 2015. ISBN 9781937513405

The Moray Firth Coastal Partnership. *Fishing for Ganseys*. Moray Firth, 2011.

Henrietta Munro & Rae Compton. *They Lived by the Sea: Folklore and Gansey Patterns of the Pentland Firth* Caithness, 1983. ISBN 0950686034

James Norbury. *Traditional Knitting Patterns from Scandinavia, the British Isles, France, Italy and Other European Countries*. Dover Publications, 1974. ISBN 9780486210131

Michael RR Pearson. *Traditional Patterns of the British Isles: Fisher Gansey-Patterns of Scotland and the Scottish Fleet*. Esteem Press, 1980. ISBN 9780906658055

Stella Ruhe. *Dutch Traditional Ganseys*. Baarn, 2013. ISBN 9058778983

Stella Ruhe. *More Traditional Dutch Ganseys*. Baarn, 2017. ISBN 9781782215080

Richard Rutt. *A History of Hand-Knitting*. Loveland, 2003. ISBN 9781931499378

Esther Rutter. *This Golden Fleece: A Journal Through Britain's Knitted History*. London, 2019. ISBN 9781783784356

Annie Shaw. *Wholegarment Knitwear: New Ways of Making Clothes*, in Text: for the Study of Textile Art, Design and History, 36, 2008-09, pp10-16

Rita Taylor, Lesley Lougher, Jan Hillier, Ken Holloway and Martin Warren. *Sheringham Ganseys: People, Places, Patterns*. Sheringham, 2017.

Henriette van der Klift-Tellegen. *Knitting from the Netherlands: Traditional Dutch Fishermen's Sweaters*. London, 1987. ISBN 0852197098

Mary Wright. *Cornish Guernseys and Knit-frocks*. Stanfords, 1979. ISBN 0906720052

Further sources

Martin Warren, Norfolk Gansey Project, www.northfolk.org.uk

Matthew Topsfield: Facebook Eriskay pattern page, www.facebook.com/KnitEriskay

Flamborough Marine Ltd, www.flamboroughmanor.co.uk/ganseys

Gansey Nation, www.ganseys.com

Ganseys, Identity Emotional Investment & Design, www.art.mmu.ac.uk/staff/research/3798

Deb Gillanders, Propagansey, www.propagansey.co.uk

Ravelry Group, www.ravelry.com/groups/guernseys-ganseys-knit-frocks---fishermens-sweaters

Sheringham Museum's 'The Gansey Page', www.sheringhammuseum.co.uk/ganseys.html

The Knitting History Forum, www.knittinghistory.co.uk

The Moray Firth Gansey Project, www.gansey-mf.co.uk/index.html

The Net Loft, www.thenetloftak.com

University of Glasgow's 'Fleece to Fashion – Economies and Cultures of Knitting in Scotland', www.gla.ac.uk/schools/humanities/research/historyresearch/researchprojects/fleece/#abouttheproject

Alexander Fenton. *Buchan Words and Ways*. 2004. Scottish Corpus of Texts & Speech. Document 1483

Rig and Furrow in Scotland, www.startrust.org.uk/RIG%20AND%20FURROW-AF.PDF

INDEX

A DAVID AND CHARLES BOOK
© David and Charles, Ltd 2021

David and Charles is an imprint of David and Charles, Ltd
Suite A, Tourism House, Pynes Hill, Exeter, EX2 5WS

Text and Designs © Di Gilpin and Sheila Greenwell 2021
Layout and Photography © David and Charles, Ltd 2021 (except images below)

Image Copyright: pages 8, 9, 10 (all photos), 16 (bottom left), 17 (top) © Scottish Fisheries Museum; pages 16 (bottom right), 17 (bottom left), 22 (photo), 140 (bottom left) © Di Gilpin; pages 11 (top images), 12 (all photos), 13 (top left, bottom left), 15 (inset photo), 17 (bottom right) © Angela Hancock; pages 20 (top) , 164 (photo) © Elena Heatherwick; page 20 (bottom) © Nick Hand

First published in the UK and USA in 2021

Di Gilpin and Sheila Greenwell have asserted their right to be identified as authors of this work in accordance with the Copyright, Designs and Patents Act, 1988.

All rights reserved. No part of this publication may be reproduced in any form or by any means, electronic or mechanical, by photocopying, recording or otherwise, without prior permission in writing from the publisher.

Readers are permitted to reproduce any of the designs in this book for their personal use and without the prior permission of the publisher. However, the designs in this book are copyright and must not be reproduced for resale.

The author and publisher have made every effort to ensure that all the instructions in the book are accurate and safe, and therefore cannot accept liability for any resulting injury, damage or loss to persons or property, however it may arise.

Names of manufacturers and product ranges are provided for the information of readers, with no intention to infringe copyright or trademarks.

A catalogue record for this book is available from the British Library.

ISBN-13: 9781446308516 paperback
ISBN-13: 9781446380383 EPUB

This book has been printed on paper from approved suppliers and made from pulp from sustainable sources.

Printed in the UK by Pureprint for:
David and Charles, Ltd
Suite A, Tourism House, Pynes Hill, Exeter, EX2 5WS

10 9 8 7 6 5 4 3 2 1

Senior Commissioning Editor: Sarah Callard
Editor: Jessica Cropper
Project Editor: Tricia Gilbert
Technical Editor: Rosee Woodland
Head of Design: Sam Staddon
Pre-press Designer: Ali Stark
Illustrations: Kuo Kang Chen & Whistlefish
Design & Art Direction: Sarah Rowntree
Photography: Jason Jenkins
Production Manager: Beverley Richardson

David and Charles publishes high-quality books on a wide range of subjects. For more information visit www.davidandcharles.com.

Layout of the digital edition of this book may vary depending on reader hardware and display settings.